A FEAST OF REASON

OR

Is Everybody Nuts But Me?

V. T. Miller

© Copyright 2009, V. T. Miller

ISBN 978-0-9788785-9-7

All rights reserved. No part of this book may be reproduced or transmitted in any form or by any means, electronic or mechanical, including photocopying, recording, or by an information storage and retrieval system, without permission in writing by the publisher.

Published by Shannon Road Press, Los Gatos, CA
www.shannonroadpress.com

Manufactured in the United States of America

DEDICATION

To Loretta; typist, editor, publisher and wife of the author. A sainted person with the inexhaustible patience and humor required to put up with it all. Also to Carp, Cromp, Heems, and Bob Powell—now departed—as well as Emmy, Stevo, Strain, Underwood, the Texas Aggie, and them, each of whom—at one time or another—caused the writer to question his sanity.

"Learned conversation is either the affectation of the ignorant or the profession of the mentally unemployed."

Oscar Wilde, "The Critic as Artist," Intentions, 1891

[Conversation is] "the feast of reason and the flow of soul."

Alexander Pope, Thoughts on Various Subjects, 1727

FOREWORD

For reasons never fully understood, I've always been fascinated by verbal communication. This interest is not so much in the transmission of information among people, but rather in what is actually said during the course of a conversation. These spoken exchanges can—and often do—range from stupefyingly banal to gut-busting funny. At some point my fascination with this phenomenon led me to take notes on various conversational encounters, which I later converted to written "dialogs."

Thus, contained herein are reasonably faithful reproductions of a number of conversations overheard or participated in by the writer (VTM, in the cast of characters) in/at various places and times over a number of years. Most of these dialogs were written during the latter part of my 29-year career with the Lockheed Missiles & Space Company in Sunnyvale, CA (circa 1980 - 86), though many were written later. This fact is of consequence only to give a time and place reference for some of the events referred to in the text.

Many of the characters in these dialogs were co-workers, friends, and relatives, and I believe that the reader's appreciation of their conversations would be enhanced if he knew these people and some of their unique characteristics. In an attempt to provide a little insight, therefore, I have provided a brief descriptive "Cast of Principal Characters," following this Foreword. Other characters are strangers whose conversations were overheard in such places as offices, restaurants, stores, and the occasional saloon. Some poetic license has been taken to facilitate presentation, though not with the conversations themselves. As noted, these conversations have been largely reconstructed from brief—but accurate—notes taken at the time (anyone here ever try to write on a wet paper bar napkin with a 2H pencil?). An exception is where the spoken part had to be assumed, such as the other end of a telephone conversation. In general, however, fidelity exists... as Huckleberry Finn said of Mark Twain in the first paragraph of his book,

> "...he told the truth, mainly. There was things which he stretched, but mainly he told the truth."

Finally, a warning to the reader. If you are a Politically Correct Person (PCP) or a candy-ass (CA), you will probably be offended by some of the inelegant language and sexist, racist, and other-ist remarks contained herein. I make no apology for this, except to note that this, too, was done in the interest of fidelity; for, as Huck went on to say, this

> "... is mostly a true book; with some stretchers, as I said before."

VTM

Los Gatos, CA
October 2009

CAST OF PRINCIPAL CHARACTERS

CO-WORKERS; FRIENDS; WIZARDS

Terry Carpenter (Carp): Intellectual wit; constant saloon companion.

Dick Crompton (Cromp): All-purpose wit; constant saloon companion.

Dave Hemmes (Heems): A little different from your average earth person. History's original software guy (need I say more?).

Steve Jerbic (Stevo): Amateur philosopher; and a guy whose view of life is somewhat skewed re that of the rest of the human race (this is not a criticism).

Lynn Jones: The East Texas Flash and Sabine County's major contribution to Texas A & M University. Noted principally for having told the truth one time in 1984.

Loretta: Co-worker; close friend; (later) girlfriend; (much later) wife.

Marv Martin: The epitome of the term "a gentleman and scholar." Owner of a small aerospace company (Command Systems Group, Inc.) for which VTM occasionally worked.

Bob Powell: A Lockheed VP and VTM's boss and mentor. Affectionately known as "Papa Bear" because, despite his intimidating presence, he killed only when necessary.

Bruce Smith: A semi-upper class Britisher (who emigrated to the U.S. in the early 70's); and a guy who *really* knows how to speak the language.

John Strain: The world's greatest test engineer; also a guy who confuses subtlety with a busted crate of live fragmentation grenades.

Emmett Taft (Emmy): A guy who has devoted the last 50 years to putting on (principally, but not limited to) the citizenry of Northern California. For many of these years he headed the Lockheed Management Association—a job for which he was paid actual money.

Bill Underwood: Fellow Oklahoman, and the "Will Rogers" of the Lockheed Missiles & Space Company.

VTM (V. Todd Miller): Caring, supportive, nurturing observer of his fellow man. Regarded by some as the "Dudley Doright" of Santa Clara County, CA; by others as a flaming sexist who is politically to the right of Alaric the Visigoth.

Tao Tao Restaurant & Bar: VTM's "Home Saloon" in Sunnyvale, CA.

- **Moi:** Inscrutable Chinese Bartender
- **Kingman:** Scrutable Chinese Bartender

TABLE OF CONTENTS

THE OFFICE

The Season of Giving	3
The Medium of Choice	5
The Twelfth Man	6
The Midnight Cyclops	8
The Clandestine Lover	9
A Time For Love	10
The Washcloth War	11
A Matter of Judgment	14
Stick & Dirt Chimneys	16
Perfidy Unmasked	18
The Female of the Species	20
The Aging Process	22
The Great Sunnyvale-Austin Data Link	23
The Invention of Wash & Wear	26
The Company Bar-B-Q	28
A Sense of Direction	30
Pragmatic Compassion	32
Hidden Treasure	33
Picturesque Speech and Patter	35
The Great Station Wagon Conversation	36
A Technology Gap	38
The Stereotype	39
The Tool of Choice	40
Singapore Lu	41
The Batting Champ	43
The Great Unwashed	44
This is My Own, My Native Land	45
School Days	47
The Importance of Faith	48
Rabbit Market Variables	49

THE HOME FRONT

Sam Houston and the Cherokees	53
The Mother's Day Gig	62
Things to Remember	64
The Cougar Crisis	66
The Bank Job	69
General Paper	72
Loretta and the Fuck Movie	74
Ear of the Beholder	79
He Sold It to Bob Stokes for Fifty Dollars	80
A Vote for Canonization	85
The Fire Giver	86
Tee Off Time	90
Great Moments in American Literature	92
If I Lived Here I'd Be Home Now	95
What Else?	97
Aristotelian Logic	98
Culture Shock	99
The Great Cone Heterodox	102

A PARALLEL UNIVERSE

Falconcrest	107
A Matter of Pronunciation	109
Cause and Effect	110
You Don't Have To Buy Nothing To Win	111
The Athenaeum Alumni Association	114
The Vicissitudes of Time	117
The Evening News	118
A Matter of Perception	120
It's Them Russians	121
Points of View	125
Adventures in Beer	127
The Essential Issue	129
Only in Ohio	131
The Death Certificate	136
Maybe It's Only An Expression	140
The All-Conference Greeter	141
A Fool And His Money	144
Relative Time	145
The Care Givers	146

THE FEMININE MYSTIQUE

Honey Vanilla	153
Assertiveness Training 101	155
Hello Dolly	156
The Austin Connection	157
Trauma	158
The Ballad of Priscilla Cotter	162
The Marilyn Monroe Fan Club	165
Pick A Number	167

A "P-DOCK" ANTHOLOGY

The Welcome Wagon	171
The Great Pie/Coffee/Carpet Caper	174
Aural Saturday	179
Rub-A-Dub-Dub	183
The Importance of Neutrality	188
Time, Temperature, Telephones, and Truck Lights	191

THE OFFICE

As the title suggests, this section is devoted to conversational encounters occurring in—or related to—what is now fashionably called "The Work Place." In spite of these dialogs, let me hasten to assure the reader that serious and important work was actually done by the personnel noted herein. In particular in such (then) esoteric areas as satellite command and control, anti-ballistic missile weapons, terrain matching guidance systems, and remotely piloted air vehicles.

The characters noted are real, the conversations really took place and are accurately quoted, but looking back, I still have trouble believing it all actually happened.

A Feast of Reason

THE OFFICE

The Season of Giving	3
The Medium of Choice	5
The Twelfth Man	6
The Midnight Cyclops	8
The Clandestine Lover	9
A Time For Love	10
The Washcloth War	11
A Matter of Judgment	14
Stick & Dirt Chimneys	16
Perfidy Unmasked	18
The Female of the Species	20
The Aging Process	22
The Great Sunnyvale-Austin Data Link	23
The Invention of Wash & Wear	26
The Company Bar-B-Q	28
A Sense of Direction	30
Pragmatic Compassion	32
Hidden Treasure	33
Picturesque Speech and Patter	35
The Great Station Wagon Conversation	36
A Technology Gap	38
The Stereotype	39
The Tool of Choice	40
Singapore Lu	41
The Batting Champ	43
The Great Unwashed	44
This is My Own, My Native Land	45
School Days	47
The Importance of Faith	48
Rabbit Market Variables	49

or, Is Everybody Nuts But Me?

THE SEASON OF GIVING

SCENE

Dick Crompton's Lockheed office, about three days before the annual Christmas break.

CHARACTERS

- Dick Crompton (Cromp)♣
- Terry Carpenter (Carp)♦ - a lifelong bachelor with no close relatives
- Steve Jerbic (Stevo)♥
- VTM♠

VTM: "Well, we've gotten through another year without having to change our names...what are you guys going to do over the holidays?"

Cromp: "Family, Christmas tree, presents, endless turkey, and all the standard crap."

Stevo: "Yeah, Jesus, what's new?"

Carp: "Well, as you guys probably know, being alone at Christmas, I usually get *myself* a really good present."

VTM: "No, I didn't know that, Carp."

♣ See CAST OF PRINCIPAL CHARACTERS
♦ Ibid.
♥ Ibid.
♠ Ibid.

3

Carp: "Yeah, it's normally something I've been wanting all year long but, for whatever reason, never took the time to buy."

Cromp: "I hope that no one here is sufficiently crass as to make a sexually-oriented comment."

Carp: *(Ignoring Crompton)* "The big problem this year, though, is that I don't know what to get myself. I've got everything a guy could possibly want...I've really studied the issue, but I still can't come up with any ideas."

Cromp: "Jesus, Carp, if that's the case, why don't you just get yourself a Gift Certificate?"

- FADE -

or, Is Everybody Nuts But Me?

THE MEDIUM OF CHOICE

SCENE

VTM's Lockheed office the day after a rare total lunar eclipse—an event carried live by most local TV stations the night before, and the subject of much discussion at Lockheed the following morning.

CHARACTERS

- Bill Underwood*
- VTM

VTM: "Well, Bill, did you watch the lunar eclipse on TV last night?"

BU: "No, but I listened to it on the radio."

- FADE -

---

* See CAST OF PRINCIPAL CHARACTERS

A FEAST OF REASON

THE TWELFTH MAN

SCENE

VTM's office at Lockheed, Sunnyvale

CHARACTERS

- Lynn Jones♣, the Legend of East Texas and a Lockheed Program Manager
- VTM

Jones: "Miller, the town I come from in Sabine County, Texas, is so little that it ain't even on the map anymore...the biggest town around there that everybody knows about is Lufkin."

VTM: *(To self)* "The mother's going to tell me another gigantic frigging lie."

Jones: "Anyway, when I was a kid, they had a big funeral for the town banker. He was a no good son of a bitch, but his wife was a nice lady, and out of respect for her, most of the townsfolk attended. The guy was such a horse's ass that they had to bring in a preacher from the next county North to say the service." *(Shelby County - ED.)*

VTM: "Jones, quit laying this rural Texas bullshit on me. I'm from Tulsa, remember? You're not talking to some California white wine drinker."

Jones: "Now, goddammit, listen to me...this is a true story."

VTM: *(To self)* "Jesus."

♣ See CAST OF PRINCIPAL CHARACTERS

Jones: "Anyway, the preacher done the best he could with the service but, in a while, he began to run down. Finally, he said to those in attendance, 'Look, most of you people knew this man a lot better than I did; maybe one of you all would like to add something to what I've said.'"

VTM: "Don't set me up, Jones."

Jones: "Well, there was a long, painful silence--seemed like it went on forever--but finally an old boy back in the corner got up and said, 'Well, if nobody here has got anything to add to the eulogy to the dear departed, I'd like to say a word or two about Texas A & M.'"

-FADE-

A Feast of Reason

THE MIDNIGHT CYCLOPS

SCENE

Around 8:00 PM at the Bold Knight—the closest saloon to Lockheed, Sunnyvale

CHARACTERS

- Dave Hemmes♣ (Heems)
- VTM

VTM: "Heems, did you ever notice that the more Dick Rose drinks, the closer his eyes get together?"

DH: "Yeah, I've noticed that. In fact, a lot of people who've seen Rose only late at night think he has only one eye."

- FADE -

♣ See CAST OF PRINCIPAL CHARACTERS

or, Is Everybody Nuts But Me?

THE CLANDESTINE LOVER

SCENE

VTM and Bill Underwood returning to Lockheed from lunch. To avoid lunchtime traffic, VTM is driving unerringly through a sprawling residential maze, characterized by many curving lanes, loops, cul-de-sacs, etc.

CHARACTERS

- Bill Underwood
- VTM

BU: *(Breaking a 5-minute silence)* "A man who knows his way through a place like this is fucking a married woman."

- FADE -

A FEAST OF REASON

A TIME FOR LOVE

SCENE

Lynn Jones's office at Lockheed's Austin, Texas, Division.

CHARACTERS

- Lynn Jones, the Wizard of College Station, Texas, and a Lockheed Program Manager
- Ralph Forest, a Lockheed Austin guy, whose girlfriend lives in Nuevo Laredo, Mexico—approximately 250 miles from Austin
- VTM

VTM: "Jesus, Jones, you oughta' get off Forest's ass about taking off early on Friday afternoons. The poor mother has to drive for over four hours before he can even get laid."

Jones: "Bullshit, Miller, that ain't no excuse. There's been many a time in my life that I had to drive for over four hours...and there was never no guarantee of any pussy at the end of the line."

- FADE -

OR, IS EVERYBODY NUTS BUT ME?

THE WASHCLOTH WAR

SCENE

VTM's Lockheed office, around 8:30 AM

CHARACTERS

- Bruce Smith[*]
- Heather (Bruce's wife, not present)
- VTM

Bruce: *(Entering office)* "Todd, I have an excruciatingly painful headache this morning."

VTM: "I'm sorry to hear that, Bruce."

B: "Yes...well, it began before I even left home this morning and is, I am confident, a direct result of a conversation I had with Heather."

VTM: "What was that, Bruce?"

B: "It was about washcloths, Todd...an incredible conversation which I will describe to you, but you must never--under any circumstances--repeat it to Heather."

VTM: "Of course not, Bruce."

B: "Well, I was in the shower this morning and reached for my washcloth, and it was not in its customary place! I then carefully opened the shower door and peered about the

---

[*] See CAST OF PRINCIPAL CHARACTERS

bathroom, and there was not a single washcloth in the entire bathroom!!"

VTM: "A washcloth gap?"

B: "Exactly."

VTM: "What steps did you take?"

B: "Well, naturally, I summoned Heather and requested an explanation...and do you know what she said?"

VTM: "I have no idea, Bruce."

B: "She said that all the washcloths had become slimy, and she was laundering them!!!"

VTM: "All at the same time?"

B: "You've hit upon the nub of the thing. I explained to her that washcloths will, in time, become slimy; the soap, at length, permeates their fabric—but, I remonstrated, that is no reason to launder every washcloth in the house simultaneously."

VTM: "To which she replied?"

B: "She said that she didn't believe that it was the soap that made them slimy—she remembered having read somewhere that washcloth sliminess owed to some other cause."

VTM: "Jesus."

B: "Exactly—well, in a desperate attempt to refocus her thoughts on the issue at hand, I pointed out that I was completely indifferent to the cause/effect relationship re washcloth sliminess and, further, that if she insisted upon laundering all the washcloths in the house at the same time, she would simply have to lay in a supply of additional washcloths as a hedge against this compulsion."

VTM: "Hot backup, day/night, all weather washcloth capability, right?"

B: "Precisely."

VTM: "And her reaction to this?"

B: "She reiterated her position--with some heat, I thought--that soap was not the culpable agent in producing washcloth sliminess--Jesus, you know, Todd, I sometimes think that you're right about women--and she further held that...."

-FADE-

A Feast of Reason

A MATTER OF JUDGMENT

SCENE

VTM and Bob Powell in San Jose airport bar, having just returned from a week-long street fight with the U.S. Air Force Space and Missile Systems Organization (SAMSO) in Los Angeles.

CHARACTERS

- Bob Powell♣
- VTM

VTM: "Jesus, I'm glad to be back. It seems like every time we go down to SAMSO for a one-day meeting, we end up spending the whole frigging week with the mothers."

BP: "Yeah, well, it just takes a little time to get through to those folks. Listen, it's early yet, finish your drink and we'll go down to the Bold Knight. Bart and Kelly and Scraggs♦ will probably be there, and we can have a couple of drinks with them."

VTM: "Jesus Christ, Bob, we've been gone for a week on what was supposed to be a one-day trip; we had three drinks at the bar at LAX, as many as we could drink during the 50 minute flight back, and four drinks here. Maybe we should begin to think in terms of going home."

♣ See CAST OF PRINCIPAL CHARACTERS
♦ Bart Morgan, Kelly Hantz, and Harold Craigs—evil companions of VTM and Powell.

BP: "That's the trouble with you, knucklehead, you don't see things clearly. That's why you'll probably never amount to anything in the Company. Look, goddammit, our wives are already pissed off at us...now there's no damn sense in wasting it."

- FADE -

A Feast of Reason

STICK & DIRT CHIMNEYS

SCENE

Lynn Jones' Lockheed office, following a brief discussion of the current price of a cord of firewood.

CHARACTERS

- Lynn Jones, Texas A & M's finest
- VTM

Jones: "Speaking of firewood, did I ever tell you about stick and dirt chimneys?"

VTM: "What?"

Jones: "Stick and dirt chimneys....Down in Sabine County, a lot of the farm houses had chimneys made of sticks and dirt--clay, actually--instead of bricks."

VTM: "Jones, don't start on me today with that East Texas bullshit."

Jones: "Goddammit, now listen to me, and you're liable to learn something. Down in that part of the state there's a kind of clay that, when you mix it with water, sets up about as hard as cement. Out in the country, people would mix this clay with little sticks *(holds out index finger to indicate size of sticks)* and build their chimneys out of that instead of bricks."

VTM: "Jesus, is there something about my appearance that automatically turns on this bullshit with you...or, maybe I've unknowingly done something bad to you in the past and you want to get even...what the hell is it?"

Jones: *(Ignoring VTM's outburst)* "Well, if you think about it, it makes a lot of sense. Sticks and dirt are a hell of a lot cheaper than bricks, and don't have to be brought in. The only problem is that you always have to build a fence around the house."

VTM: *(Hitting the bait)* "Why is that?"

Jones: "Well, the particular kind of clay they have down there has a high salt content, and if they don't fence off the houses, the cows come in and lick the chimneys down."

VTM: "Goddamn you Jones...don't you have any work to do? How much time do you spend thinking up this shit?"

Jones: *(Undeterred)* "In fact, I've heard that sometimes pregnant women would get in and lick the chimneys, but I never put a whole lot of faith in...."

- FADE -

A Feast of Reason

PERFIDY UNMASKED

SCENE

Circa 1962, the Brass Rail saloon around 6:00 PM, following a long day working the Satellite Tracking Net at Lockheed.

CHARACTERS

- David Hemmes (Heems)
- VTM

DH: "It's becoming more and more clear to me that this whole thing has been faked...there's nothing real about any part of it."

VTM: "What whole thing?"

DH: "Lockheed...the whole company—it's not real, it's a gigantic farce."

VTM: "I never realized that."

DH: "You notice all the new buildings springing up around the Lockheed complex? I don't think they're real buildings... think they're only cardboard cutout facades, held up from behind by 2 x 4's...like on the MGM back lot."

VTM: "Jesus...we'll have to look behind some of them."

DH: "The people aren't real either—they're not Lockheed employees, or even aerospace people—they're all from Central Casting."

VTM: "You may have something there...I sure know some guys who aren't real anything."

DH: "You're not real either, Miller--you're not an engineer, you're also from Central Casting. You've been taught a few engineering words and technical phrases just to mislead me-- it's all a gigantic practical joke."

VTM: "What do you suppose the purpose of this conspiracy is?"

DH: "It's a plot to drive me out of my mind...and it's working--but I'll tell you one thing about the guy behind it."

VTM: "What's that?"

DH: "It's costing him a bundle."

- FADE -

A Feast of Reason

THE FEMALE OF THE SPECIES

SCENE

VTM's Lockheed office.

CHARACTERS

- Steve Jerbic
- VTM

SJ: "Todd, do you know anything about growing marijuana?"

VTM: "No, Stevo, I've never screwed around much with marijuana. I've always figured that booze gives me all the trouble I can handle....Why? What's the problem?"

SJ: "Well, I want to plant some marijuana, but I want to get ahold of a female plant because I hear that they produce a lot higher quality leaves than the male bush. The problem is that I don't know how to tell the difference between the two."

VTM: "I don't know what the difference is either, Stevo, but I would guess that the female is probably the dumber of the two."

- SEXIST LAUGHTER -

— Several days later in Tao Tao bar

SJ: "Well, I got my marijuana planted, and I was able to get a female plant."

OR, IS EVERYBODY NUTS BUT ME?

VTM: "How do you know it's a female?"

SJ: "I asked it some questions."

- FADE -

A Feast of Reason

THE AGING PROCESS

SCENE

Lynn Jones' Lockheed office...late on a Friday afternoon.

CHARACTERS

- Lynn Jones
- VTM

VTM: "The weekend is finally coming up...what are you gonna' do tomorrow?"

LJ: "I've got to go get some lumber, in connection with a project I've got going at home."

VTM: "Jesus; that sounds exciting."

LJ: "Well, at my age, it ain't really all that bad. A man can tell that he's getting old when, on a Saturday, he'd rather go down to Southern Lumber and look at boards than he would chase pussy."

- FADE -

OR, IS EVERYBODY NUTS BUT ME?

THE GREAT SUNNYVALE-AUSTIN DATA LINK

SCENE

FAX machine area outside VTM's Sunnyvale Office; VTM in office.

CHARACTERS

- "Cush" Cushman
- FAX Machine
- Female Person on Austin End of FAX Machine (FP)
- VTM

Cush: *(On phone to FP)* "Yes...yes, I can hear you now, but I couldn't there for a while."

FP: *(VTM assumes)* "I can hear you okay, too."

C: "I've been trying to get ahold of you all morning–I guess no one was in your FAX area this morning–Ha, Ha!"

VTM: *(To self)* "Mother of God."

C: "Oh, you were there, huh....Well, I just assumed you were gone, knowing you Austin people...Ha, Ha!!"

VTM: *(To self)* "Why doesn't that fuckhead just FAX his stuff...why do the mothers always have to talk to each other over the phone at the same time?"

C: "No, I just sent Page 4...I sent Page 3 when we talked yesterday–remember?"

FP: *(VTM assumes)* "Well, I'm not receiving anything."

C: "Well, it's transmitting at this end. It can't fall off in between."

VTM: *(To self)* "It can if you've got anything to do with the operation, Cush."

FP: *(VTM assumes)* "Well, I'm not receiving anything."

C: "It should be coming through...my Transmitter Light is on."

VTM: *(To self)* "Underwood is right...you could give that asshole a ten-penny nail, and he'd work all day with it."

C: "Oh, it is?–Good–If at first you don't succeed...Ha, Ha!!!"

VTM: *(To self)* "I'm going to kill that simple shit."

C: "Oh, your Receive Switch was...Right, well I thought something was fishy."

VTM: "Jesus."

C: "You have all of Page 4 now? Well, a bird in the hand is worth two in the bush."

VTM: *(Patience exhausted)* "Cush, goddammit, can't you just FAX that shit without holding a fucking Talk Show with the Austin broad?"

—*Sounds of Madam Fong (VTM's secretary) leaving desk because of 'Test Base' language*—

C: "Well the problem was that, while my Transmit Light was on, her Receive Switch was..."

VTM: *(Interrupting)* "I don't give a shit about that, Cush. Why don't you assholes just shove the fucking paper in the machine without all the bullshit conversation?"

C: "Well, first, you've got to understand how the FAX machine works....Let me explain...."

-FADE-

A Feast of Reason

THE INVENTION OF WASH & WEAR

SCENE

In car driving from SAMSO (see <u>A Matter of Judgment</u>) near LAX to hotel in Manhattan Beach, CA, on fourth day of a one-day trip.

CHARACTERS

- Bob Powell
- Dave Hemmes
- Bill (Speeder) Loo
- VTM

BP: "I'm either gonna' have to get some laundry done or buy some shirts and skivvies. I'm completely out of clean clothes."

VTM: "I don't know where the hell we're going to buy any clothes at 7:30 PM. We'd have been all right if you hadn't kept the frigging meeting going forever...as usual."

BP: "Oh shut up, for Christ's sake. If you'd take a little more interest in running the engineering end of the program, then I wouldn't have to...etc." *(Public excoriation of VTM follows).*

DH: "Listen, you guys, Speeder Loo can do our laundry--being Chinese he understands that kind of stuff."

SL: "Goddamn, you mothers are funny."

BP: "Well, let's get to the hotel and drop off all this stuff in the rooms. We can meet in the bar in about an hour."

Later—VTM in hotel room when Powell calls on phone.

BP: "I've been reading the label on one of my dirty shirts, and it says that a man can wash the shirt, hang it up to dry, and then wear it without ironing."

VTM: "Yeah, it's called a wash and wear shirt."

BP: "Listen, goddammit, it says you can wash the shirt anywhere—like in a hotel bathroom—and put it on when it's dry."

VTM: "Yeah, the shirt's geographically independent...it doesn't give a shit where you wash it."

BP: "Goddammit, knucklehead, if you'd ever get over that frigging smartass attitude of yours, you might just learn something. The trouble with you is that nobody can ever tell you a goddamn thing, and that's why...etc."

- FADE -

A Feast of Reason

THE COMPANY BAR-B-Q

SCENE

Lynn Jones' Lockheed office, discussing the Bar-B-Q'ing of a whole pig. An event that Jones has been planning for several months.

CHARACTERS

- Lynn Jones
- Dick Crompton
- Terry Carpenter
- VTM
- Rhoda Cruz—A Lockheed secretary, built somewhat along the lines of the Michelin Man.

VTM: "So, when are you going to stop screwing around, Jones, and Bar-B-Q the pig?"

Jones: "Godammit, I'm ready to go, except that I haven't been able to find the right kind of pig. It has to be a certain size and have the right amount of fat on it."

Cromp: "Pig? Hell, if it's fat you want, why piss away money buying a pig? Why don't you guys just Bar-B-Q Rhoda?"

VTM: "That's not bad, Cromp."

Carp: "Well, I've got to tell you guys that if you want to cook Rhoda, you'd better get with it. She's been on a diet for the past week or so, and she's losing succulence every day."

- FADE -

A Feast of Reason

A SENSE OF DIRECTION

SCENE

In car in Arlington, VA, headed for Arlington Hall (then, home of U. S. Army Intelligence and Security Command - INSCOM) to give a major briefing to Army personnel, including several generals. Also attending are the CEO of the Lockheed Corporation, and the President of Lockheed Missiles & Space Company.

CHARACTERS

- Bruce Smith
- VTM

Bruce: "Jesus, Todd, it's quarter of eight, and the meeting's at eight o'clock...I thought you knew the way to Arlington Hall."

VTM: "I do, goddammit, I just made a wrong turn somewhere."

Bruce: "We simply must be on time, Todd...I know that there will be at least five generals at the meeting, plus all the Lockheed brass...and you and I must give the major portion of the briefing."

VTM: "I know all that, Bruce. Stick with me—I know this area like the back of my hand."

—Another ten minutes of fruitless driving ensues—

Bruce: "Jesus, Todd, maybe we should ask someone for directions."

VTM: "Bullshit, Bruce, we're getting close...I can tell."

Bruce: "Todd, it's almost eight o'clock and you and I are first up at the briefing. We simply must—Look! There's a chap on the curb ahead—pull over and I'll ask him for directions."

VTM: "Oh, all right, for Christ's sake...Jesus, what a candy ass you are."

—pulls over to curb—

Bruce: *(To local citizen)* "I say, we seem to have lost our way. I wonder if you could direct us to Arlington Hall?"

LC: "Nynn...I hnn just moved hnn to Hnarlington hnn last wheek, so I'm not too famhiliar with the hnn area."

VTM: *(To self)* "Jesus, the guy's a frigging *harelip*."

Bruce: *(to LC)* "Quite...yes, well, thank you very much."

VTM *(Pulling away from curb)* "Jesus Christ, Smith, how the fuck could you pick the only transient *harelip* in Northern Virginia to ask directions from?"

Bruce: "I don't believe that he is a *harelip*, Todd...I think that his speaking problem owes more to a cleft palate, and further that...."

- FADE -

A Feast of Reason

PRAGMATIC COMPASSION

SCENE

Dick Crompton's office, Lockheed Sunnyvale, Monday morning.

CHARACTERS

- Crompton
- Terry Carpenter
- VTM

Cromp: "I hear Paul Haggett died over the weekend."

VTM: "That's right."

Carp: "How did it happen?"

VTM: "It happened Saturday at the annual Engineering Picnic. He was playing doubles tennis and had a heart attack on the court...apparently he died almost instantly."

Cromp: "What happened to his tennis racquet?"

VTM: "Wha'd'ya mean 'What happened to his tennis racquet?'"

Cromp: "Well, we could sell it. We could run an ad in the *Lockheed Star*:

'Tennis racquet; nearly new; dropped once.'"

- FADE -

or, Is Everybody Nuts But Me?

HIDDEN TREASURE

SCENE

Lunch time at Tao Tao bar.

CHARACTERS

- Lynn Jones (the Absolute Aggie)
- VTM

LJ: *(Out of nowhere)* "Miller, I had an uncle who was an alcoholic, and his wife was always getting on his ass about his drinking."

VTM: *(To self)* "Jesus, here it comes again." *(To LJ)* "That right?"

LJ: "Yeah...well he used to hide his bottles so she couldn't get 'em and pour 'em out, but gradually she would find all his hidin' places."

VTM: "Jones, why are you telling me this shit?"

LJ: "Now, listen to me, godammit...anyway, he had one place she never found--he hung his bottles down the chimney on strings, but high enough up so they couldn't be seen in the fireplace."

VTM: "For Christ's sake, Lynn, stop it--will you?"

LJ: "Well, of course, his whole scheme collapsed when the first fire was lit that fall...it *was* fairly spectacular, though."

VTM: *(To self)* "Mother of God."

LJ: "Anyway, he was pretty old by that time, and about half senile–in fact, it wasn't long after that we had to tuck him away in *'The Home'*."

VTM: "I can't bear this."

LJ: "The final tip-off came the day he hid a quart of bourbon under the living room rug."

- FADE -

or, Is Everybody Nuts But Me?

PICTURESQUE SPEECH AND PATTER

SCENE

A stormy winter day–heavy rain, high winds, thunder, etc. VTM and Doug Prins driving from Gilroy to Sunnvale, CA (reason forgotten).

CHARACTERS

- Doug Prins–New to northern California, having just moved from the East Coast
- VTM

Prins: "Jesus, what a storm. Look at that rain out over the hills."

VTM: "Yeah, that's the way winter is in northern California--constant rain."

Prins: "Shit, it's not just the rain...listen to that wind...we're frigging doomed."

VTM: "Bullshit, Prins--it's just a normal winter day for this area."

Prins: "Normal, my ass. This is the kind of shit that sucked up the little cunt in the *Wizard of Oz*."

-FADE-

A Feast of Reason

THE GREAT STATION WAGON CONVERSATION

SCENE

Command Systems Group, Inc., Conference Room, waiting for meeting to convene.

CHARACTERS

- Marv Martin♣
- Chuck Franklin, an electronics, computer, autopilot guy (all weird) and, in the 1970's, probably the only hippie in California who wore designer jeans and drove a Cadillac Sedan de Ville.
- VTM
- Others

VTM: "Marv, I finally finished refurbishing that old '73 Mercury station wagon of mine...had it painted a couple of weeks ago, and it really looks great...came out a lot better than I expected."

Marv: "Shirley and I found out that the baby's going to be a boy. As you probably know, nowadays a baby's sex can be determined before birth, and it's going to be a boy."

VTM: *(To self)* "What the hell's that got to do with my paint job?"

Marv: "We also learned that the baby will be born in October, though there's some disagreement about the exact date. The USC doctor says the 15th, but Shirley's Ob/Gyn thinks it will be closer to the 30th."

♣ See CAST OF PRINCIPAL CHARACTERS

VTM: *(To self)* "Goddammit, I wanted to tell about my station wagon."

Marv: "An earlier birth is preferable, of course, even if labor must be induced."

Chuck: *(Adding fuel to fire)* "Why is that, Marv?"

Marv: "Well, with women Shirley's age, there are sometimes complications near the end of pregnancy. The earlier birth, of course, reduces this risk. Moreover, it's beneficial from the standpoint of ...."

- FADE -

A TECHNOLOGY GAP

SCENE

VTM and the College Station Comet leaving Lockheed for lunch, driving up Bayshore Freeway.

CHARACTERS

- Lynn Jones
- VTM

VTM: "I wish these silly assholes would get the hell out of the way when I'm trying to get somewhere."

LJ: "For Christ's sake, Miller, will you quit your constant bitching about the traffic?"

VTM: "The mothers all have 40 mph brains in a 70 mph world."

LJ: "That may be, but you're just going to have to put up with it."

VTM: "Whaddya' mean, I'm going to have to put up with it?"

LJ: "Just the same way you're going to have to put up with women...until some smart guy comes along and figures out how to hang snatches on fence posts."

-FADE-

or, Is Everybody Nuts But Me?

THE STEREOTYPE

SCENE

Lockheed Building 578 Conference Room, circa 1983

CHARACTERS

- Bill Underwood, wearing a brand new pair of light tan Hush Puppies
- Lynn Jones, the Texas Aggie All-Star
- VTM

Jones: "Underwood, if it wasn't for smokes and Okies, they wouldn't sell a single pair of them damn Hush Puppies."

- FADE -

THE TOOL OF CHOICE

SCENE

Lunch time, Tao Tao bar.

CHARACTERS

- Lynn Jones, Texas A & M's Own
- VTM

LJ: "I'm goddamned sick and tired of hearing the Mexican migrant workers pissing and moaning about having to use those short-handled hoes in the field."

VTM: "What's the issue?"

LJ: "They say using a short-handled hoe day after day causes severe back problems."

VTM: "Yeah, I can see how it would."

LJ: "Well, shit, it's not our fault. Those short-handled hoes are a Mexican invention. The migrants brought 'em in when they came into the U.S. Christ's sake, even a cotton choppin' field hand has sense enough to use a long-handled Scovill."

-FADE-

or, Is Everybody Nuts But Me?

SINGAPORE LU

SCENE

VTM's office in a closed area of Lockheed Sunnyvale Building 102; early 1960's.

CHARACTERS

- VTM
- Miss Lu Hugdahl, VTM's secretary and friend--a delightful lady, who projects a continuous aura of vague preoccupation, as though (perhaps) hearing voices from deep space.
- A highly-placed civilian visitor from the USAF Foreign Technology Division (VTM's customer), Wright-Patterson AFB, Dayton, Ohio. Visitor is dressed in a conservative suit and tie (but, in the Midwestern fashion of the day, with large garish tie bar). Because of the visitor, VTM also wears a conservative suit and tie (unusual), though the latter features a small elasticized emblem which, when stretched out, spells "FUCK YOU" in tasteful multi-colored script.

VTM: *(Adopting the pseudo-formality which he and Miss Hugdahl often employ to suck in strangers)* "Thank you, Miss Hugdahl, for bringing in the coffee."

MH: *(With practiced equal formality)* "You're most welcome, Mr. Miller. Will there be anything else?"

VTM: "I believe not, Miss Hugdahl, although you might stay, in case there is a need for note taking."

MH: "I'll be glad to be of help, Mr. Miller."

VTM: *(Sensing that the FTD visitor is your basic Mk. I Civil Service Numb Nuts)* "Dr. (name forgotten), you wouldn't think it from her demeanor, but Miss Hugdahl commands a considerable local reputation as a sensual—one could even say provocative—interpretive dancer...in fact, she's known throughout the Program as 'Singapore Lu.' Perhaps you can give Dr. (?) a brief sampler, Miss Hugdahl."

MH: *(With regret)* "Oh, I'm terribly sorry, Mr. Miller, but I dropped off my seven veils at the dry cleaners just this morning."

VTM: "Well, you could use seven old inter-departmental memos, Miss Hugdahl. In fact, the onion skin flimsies would do nicely."

FTDV: *(Who has developed a perceptible tic under his left eye)* "Yes, well, perhaps some other time. My schedule is quite full today, and there are several fairly complex technical issues which I must discuss with you."

VTM: "OK, but if you could hang in for lunch afterwards, there's a sensational amateur topless joint just across the highway, and the three of us could...."

- FADE -

or, Is Everybody Nuts But Me?

THE BATTING CHAMP

SCENE

Circa 1968, the Bold Knight restaurant (the closest saloon to Lockheed), around 6:00 PM. A brief discussion of the San Francisco Giants' chances in the National League West has just concluded.

CHARACTERS

- VTM
- Kelly Hantz   )
- Bart Morgan   )♣
- Harold Craigs)

KH: "Speaking of baseball, I was a pretty nifty little infielder in college."

VTM: "Bullshit, Hantz, the most athletic game you ever played is Nine-Ball."

KH: "Whaddya' mean 'Bullshit'? I lettered two years in baseball at Oklahoma A&M...in fact, I'd be in the majors today but some cocksucker came along and invented the curve ball."

-FADE-

♣ See A Matter of Judgment

A Feast of Reason

THE GREAT UNWASHED

SCENE

Bini's restaurant located in the cannery district of San Jose, CA. Bini's is housed in an old ramshackle wooden structure adjacent to a railroad siding and has, over the years, become something of a local legend. Because of this, Bini's attracts an eclectic group of customers consisting of cannery workers, stock brokers, construction personnel, lawyers, business men, police officers, etc.♣

CHARACTERS

- The Texas Aggie
- VTM

L. Jones: *(To VTM, upon entering the restaurant):* "Look at these dumb bastards, Miller. Not one of 'em has ever had to write an aerospace proposal."

-FADE-

♣ And also because martinis are served in milk shake cans.

or, Is Everybody Nuts But Me?

THIS IS MY OWN, MY NATIVE LAND

SCENE

VTM's Lockheed Office, circa 1968.

CHARACTERS

- Troy Wayne (Tex) Whitfield
- VTM

Tex: "You know, my wife's from Oklahoma, so we have to go back there every couple of years to see her folks."

VTM: "Yeah, that's about what I do."

Tex: "We usually drive back, rather than fly, because we have so many places to go when we get there."

VTM: "That's what I do, too, when I have the time."

Tex: "I usually make it in two days because I drive long hours...I don't like to stop once I get going."

VTM: "That right?"

Tex: "Yeah, but I can always tell when we cross the Oklahoma state line--even if it's in the middle of the night."

VTM: "How's that?"

Tex: "I get a hard-on, and start looking around for something to steal."

- FADE -

or, Is Everybody Nuts But Me?

SCHOOL DAYS

SCENE

VTM's Lockheed office, around 5:00 PM, BS'ing with the Sabine County Whiz.

CHARACTERS

- Lynn Jones
- VTM

LJ: "Miller, I know that you know Tex Whitfield, but did you ever meet his wife?"

VTM: "No, I never did."

LJ: "Well, she's an Oklahoma girl...probably somewhere in her mid 50's by now...and next September she's starting college, as a Freshman."

VTM: "How come her to want to start college at that age?"

LJ: "I don't know...just got tired of being ignorant, I reckon."

- FADE -

THE IMPORTANCE OF FAITH

SCENE

Doyle Mattson and VTM having lunch at a restaurant near Lockheed.

CHARACTERS

- Doyle Mattson—Chief Test Engineer of Lockheed's Missile Systems Division and VTM's current boss. Also a Christian Scientist who, in keeping with his religion, is a non-drinker. Despite this failing, Doyle is regarded as a first class guy by all who know him.
- VTM

DM: "For years I've had this recurring dream in which I'm running naked down the main street of some urban area or, maybe, a small town."

VTM: "Jesus, Doyle, that Christian Science stuff doesn't seem to be working too well for you."

DM: "The hell it isn't—I haven't been caught yet."

-FADE-

or, Is Everybody Nuts But Me?

RABBIT MARKET VARIABLES

SCENE

Two retirees having a couple of drinks at La Hacienda Inn–a local watering place.

CHARACTERS

- Bob Powell (See <u>A Matter of Judgment</u> and <u>The Invention of Wash and Wear</u>.)
- VTM

BP: *(Horatio Alger-ing VTM)* "Well, I was born and raised on a farm in western Tennessee♣...we were quite a ways from the nearest town♦, so we didn't have indoor plumbing or electricity...had a privy out back and coal oil lamps in the house."

VTM: *(To self)* "Where's Lynn Jones when I need him?"

BP: "When I got a little older, though, I could always make a little spending money trapping rabbits."

VTM: "Trapping rabbits?"

BP: "Yeah...I'd trap 'em and gut 'em and sell them to the grocery store in town for 15 cents each."

VTM: "Jesus, that doesn't sound like much money."

♣ For you Yankees, this is properly pronounced TENNA - *see*.
♦ Milan, TN (Ed.)

BP: "Yeah, but these were 'hill rabbits'...you could get a little more for 'swamp rabbits'—maybe 20 cents or so. The problem was that most swamp rabbits were farther west—toward the river."

VTM: "How come you could get more money for a swamp rabbit than for a hill rabbit?"

BP: "Well, a swamp rabbit is about 30 percent bigger than a hill rabbit."

VTM: "How come 'em to be bigger?"

BP: "Well they have bigger bones, a bigger frame, and more meat on 'em."

VTM: "I understand that, but *why* is a swamp rabbit bigger than a hill rabbit?"

BP: "I don't know...maybe swampy land provides more food or nourishment for the rabbit...or maybe it's just a healthier environment for 'em."

VTM: "Well, I'd think that living on a hill would be a lot healthier than living in a swamp."

BP: "Why don't you drink your goddamn drink?"

-FADE-

or, Is Everybody Nuts But Me?

THE HOME FRONT

The conversations detailed herein occurred mostly among the writer, his wife, son, mother, and other assorted relatives. While I want to believe that my family is semi-normal in most respects, still, I occasionally wonder if their collective elevator goes all the way to the top.

THE HOME FRONT

Sam Houston and the Cherokees	53
The Mother's Day Gig	62
Things to Remember	64
The Cougar Crisis	66
The Bank Job	69
General Paper	72
Loretta and the Fuck Movie	74
Ear of the Beholder	79
He Sold It to Bob Stokes for Fifty Dollars	80
A Vote for Canonization	85
The Fire Giver	86
Tee Off Time	90
Great Moments in American Literature	92
If I Lived Here I'd Be Home Now	95
What Else?	97
Aristotelian Logic	98
Culture Shock	99
The Great Cone Heterodox	102

OR, IS EVERYBODY NUTS BUT ME?

SAM HOUSTON AND THE CHEROKEES

SCENE

In automobile traveling from Uncle Walter's house on Texas side of Lake Texhoma to Lake Texhoma Lodge (for dinner) on Oklahoma side of Lake--a distance of approximately 20 miles. Car is nearing end of bridge over lake, approaching Oklahoma.

CHARACTERS

- VTM
- Vista, VTM's Mother (age 75 and arbiter of local morals and mores)
- Uncle Walter, Patriarch of the clan (age 91, ex-lawyer, ex-Speaker of Oklahoma House of Representatives, ex-judge, deaf in one ear, and holder of strong opinions)
- Aunt Alice, Walter's wife (age 86, lame, historian and curator of all family affairs, and one of the great talkers of our time)

Vista: "Now, Todd, watch the 55 mile an hour speed limit--they don't give you any cushion in Oklahoma."

VTM: "Right, Mother."

AA: "Now, watch the speed limit in Oklahoma, Todd--they don't...*etc.* "

UW: "You better set that cruise control at 55--they don't...*etc.*"

VTM: *(To self)* "Jesus Christ, am I going to have to listen to this shit for 20 miles?"

V: "Up here about 12 miles, we've got to turn right on State Route 32 and go through Kingston to the Lodge."

UW: "There's a flashing red light at the junction...you hit that and just bend her East, some."

VTM: *(Having been down this road about 10^6 times in the past)* "I know how to get to the Lodge."

V: "You knew that good shortcut to Pawhuska that time, too."

VTM: "Jesus, Mother, that was in 1947."

V: "It never hurts to remember those things...you've never been exactly eat up with humility...*pride goeth before a fall.*"

AA: "'*A man's pride shall bring him low, but honor shall uphold the humble in spirit*'...Proverbs 29:23."

VTM: *(Under breath)* "I'm fucking going to kill somebody before this is over."

LATER

V: "There's the flashing light; that's Highway 32; turn right at the light."

AA: "Up yonder's the turn off, Todd."

UW: "Turn East at the light, and it's about four miles to Kingston, then about four more to the Lodge."

VTM: *(To self)* "It's too bad these three mothers weren't helping the Navigation Officer on the Titanic that night." *(Turns right—East—on to Route 32 at flashing red light.)*

V: "Now, it's about five miles to Kingston."

UW: "Four."

AA: "How far is it to Kingston?"

UW: *(Approaching Kingston, Oklahoma)* "The best Governor the State of Oklahoma ever had was born right here in this town."

VTM: "Who was that, Uncle Walter?"

UW: "Raymond Geary."

VTM: "I think he was Governor when I left Oklahoma to come to California--either Geary or the guy before him--who was Governor before Geary?"

UW: "Johnston Murray, and he was the sorriest Governor the state ever had."

V: "Todd, there's a drugstore in Kingston; I need to get some cigarettes."

VTM: "OK, Mother, I'll stop."

V: "You don't know where it is."

AA: "See that yellow house over yonder, Walter? That's where Sue Ann lives, that works at the *rest home* in Whitesboro."

VTM: "I know where the drugstore is; I was in there the last time I was home."

UW: "They indicted him for fraud right after he left office."

V: "They built the drugstore since then."

VTM:	*(Trying to change subject)* "Who was Governor before Johnston Murray, Uncle Walter?"
UW:	"Roy Turner, and before him was Bob Kerr, and before him..."
V:	"You sure triggered something now."
UW:	"...was Bill Marlin, and before ..."
AA:	"Turn in! Turn in! There's the drugstore."
V:	"Turn left--there's the drugstore."
VTM:	*(Who has had the drugstore in sight for four blocks)* "I see it, gang." *(Turns in.)*
UW:	"...him was Red Phillips, and ..."
AA:	"Todd, Miriam that was married to your Uncle Claude lived here in Kingston for a while."
VTM:	"That right?"
AA:	"Yes, but that was after Claude was taken."
UW:	"...before him was Bill Murray--he was Johnston Murray's father--and..."
VTM:	*(To self)* "Jesus, he's going to go all the way back to the Territorial Governors."
V:	"I've got the cigarettes--let's go on to the Lodge--and watch the speed limit."

AA: "Watch that *Endin* over there—he'll step right out in front of you."

UW: "...before him—well, it wouldn't be no great loss if we ran over that *Endin*—unless it dented up the car."

V: "Walter, you shouldn't talk that way about Indians."

UW: "Well, there may be a gas shortage, but there's no clear and present danger of running shy of *Endins*—at least not in Oklahoma...and before Bill Murray was William Haskell. Now, Haskell was a Territorial Governor..."

VTM: *(To self)* "I knew it; I frigging knew it." *(Trying to change subject)* "Where was Johnston Murray from, Uncle Walter?"

UW: "Okmulgee...and the Governor before him—Turner—was from Ardmore, and the Governor before him..."

VTM: *(To self)* "Jesus, I've done it again."

UW: "...was from Oklahoma City, and before him was from Tishomingo, and before him..."

GOES BACK TO TERRITORIAL GOVERNORS AGAIN

"...now, Haskell wasn't even born in the Territory—he come from Missouri, originally. He caught his wife in a compromisin' position with another man and come West."

VTM: "Uncle Walter, can you do the Governors by height?"

V: "No, but he can probably do 'em by hat size."

UW: "Now, a similar thing happened to Sam Houston."

V: "What was that, Walter?"

UW: "He caught his wife a-triflin' with another man, so he resigned his office in Tennessee and taken off to live with the Cherokees for two years."

VTM: *(To self)* "Mother of God."

AA: "How come him to do that? It looks to me like he had enough trouble without goin' to live with the *Endins*."

UW: *(By way of clarification)* "Well, that was before he come to Texas."

AA: "Todd, you remember Buck Cartwright that run for office against Walter that time...well, he's been bad sick for a long time...had to have a place taken off of his face...but he's all right, now."

V: "Shirley—that's his wife—is still in that *home* up in Wewoka, though."

AA: "Isn't that the most pathetic thing about Shirley? She don't even know Buck half the time nomore."

UW: "See that blue sign up there? That's the turn off to the Lodge...take her easy though, there's a bad culvert going in."

VTM: "Why don't I drop you all off at the door, and I'll go park the car."

AA: "All right, but you'll have to help me out...I've got the *arthuritis* so bad I can barely get up and down."

VTM: *(Later, entering dining room after having parked the car)* "Did you all get a waitress yet?"

UW: "No, but here comes one now."

Waitress: "You folks want to see menus?"

VTM: "No, we just come in to watch the murals for a while."

V: "Todd, I wish you'd get rid of some of that California smart mouth."

UW: "What do you want, Alice?"

AA: "I'd like to have the chicken fried steak, but it gives me indigestion so bad..."

UW: "With cows, they call it the bloat."

AA: "No cow never got it from eatin' chicken fried steak."

VTM: "Chicken fried steak-fed cows do."

V: "I'm not going to tell you again, Todd."

AA: *(After orders are placed)* "Todd, it's too bad you won't be here next week...James—that's Charles' youngest boy—is coming in for a couple of days."

VTM: "That right? I haven't seen James since he was little...what's he doing now?"

AA: "He works on computers, someway."

VTM: "Who does he work for?"

AA: "He works for the Chevrolet Company down in Dallas, except for one night a week when he works for the Methodists."

VTM: "The Methodists? What Methodists?"

AA: "The ones down in Dallas…that run that college."

VTM: "You mean Southern Methodist University?"

AA: "That sounds right."

UW: "I'll say one thing about SMU, after about 15 years of being down, they had a right fair ball club last year…they were getting' about as sorry as Texas Christian."

V: "You talk about sorry, you got to say something about Rice."

VTM: "How are the Sooners going to do this fall, Uncle Walter?"

UW: "Well, if that boy they've had Redshirted pans out at quarterback, and they can come up with just one good outside spook, they'll be back in Miami on New Years' Day."

V: "You're supposed to call them Blacks nowadays, Walter."

UW: "Brain surgeons are Blacks; running backs are spooks."

VTM: "Well, since we've finished dinner, why don't I bring the car around?"

AA: "You bring the car around, Todd, your Uncle Walter and I are just give out."

OR, IS EVERYBODY NUTS BUT ME?

UW: "Bring the car around, Todd, and we'll just retrace our steps on Route 32 back to Kingston, and then..."

VTM: *(To self, retreating from dining room)* "Mother of Christ—I can't bear it—my whole goddamned family is from Central Casting...I'm going to go live with the fucking Cherokees."

- FADE -

A Feast of Reason

THE MOTHER'S DAY GIG

SCENE

VTM's house on a weekday evening.

CHARACTERS

- Loretta♣
- VTM

Loretta: "Listen, my son is coming down from Vallejo this weekend to spend Mother's Day with me."

VTM: "That right?"

L: "Yes, and I'm going to fix a nice dinner at my place on Saturday evening–would you like to come over?"

VTM: "No, I don't think so, Babe–Mother's Day is kind of a family thing."

L: "No, really, it would be no extra work, and I'd like to have you."

VTM: "Well thanks, Babe, but I've got a lot of stuff to do around the house this weekend."

L: "You never come over to my place anymore."

VTM: "Whadda'ya' mean I never come over to your place anymore?"

L: "You just never come over to my apartment anymore."

♣ See CAST OF PRINCIPAL CHARACTERS

VTM: "Well, I haven't been keeping score, but it seems to me that I've been by a few times in recent history."

L: "You never come over anymore."

VTM: "Well, if it's that frigging important to you, then—sure, I'd like to come over."

L: "Well, you don't have to if you don't want to..."

- FADE -

A Feast of Reason

THINGS TO REMEMBER

SCENE

VTM's living room; VTM watching college football game on TV

CHARACTERS

- VTM
- VTM's mother (Vista)
- Loretta
- Loretta's mother (Opal)
- Others

Loretta : *(Reading ads in San Francisco Chronicle)* "Why, here's a skirt I'd sure like to buy, but I don't think I can get it in my size."

Vista : "Why, Loretta, you don't look more than a size 12 to me."

L : "No, I'm a 14."

V : "Well, you sure don't look more than a 12."

Opal : "Loretta's a bigger woman than she looks."

V : "Well, she doesn't look more than a 12."

L : "No, even after losing all that weight, I'm still more comfortable in a 14."

V : "Well, I'd never have figured you for more than a 12."

L : "No, I'm a 14."

OR, IS EVERYBODY NUTS BUT ME?

O :   "No, she's a 14."

VTM :   *(To self)* "How in Christ's name can things like this happen in my own home? A guy tries to watch a frigging football game, and...etc."

- FADE -

A Feast of Reason

THE COUGAR CRISIS

SCENE I

VTM's house, the Sunday of a Memorial Day weekend.

CHARACTERS

- Loretta
- VTM
- Chris (VTM's 11 year old kid)

Loretta: *(Entering house from car, and crying)* "Oh, Todd...SOB, SNIFF..."

VTM: "What's the matter, Loretta?"

L: "I just scraped the–SNIFF–fender on my new car."

VTM: "Jesus–the new car? How the hell did you do that?"

L: "On that stupid garage at my house–SOB, SNIFF."

VTM: *(A picture of sympathy)* "Jesus that's dumb...you scraped the fender on your old car the same way two or three times."

L: "I know it...I just can't bear it."

VTM: "Christ sake, it seems to me that, after a while, even a broad could learn to..."

L: "It's not my fault–the garage is too narrow...especially with a car parked on the other side."

or, Is Everybody Nuts But Me?

VTM : "Bullshit, Loretta, Helen Keller could park a frigging refrigerator truck in that garage."

Chris : "Boy, she really screwed it up, too!! I was there!!"

L : "Shut up, Chris."

VTM : "Well, let me go take a look at the mother...maybe I can...."

SCENE II *(ASSUMED)*

McHugh Lincoln/Mercury, Los Gatos, the Tuesday after the Memorial Day weekend.

CHARACTERS

- Service Manager
- Body Shop Foreman

SM : "Ernie, you remember that broad that come in last Friday evening and picked up the new blue Cougar?"

BSF : "The one with the big tits?"

SM : "No, the one that picked up the *dark* blue Cougar."

BSF : "Oh yeah–the older broad with the cigarette holder."

SM : "Well, she come back today...already scraped a fender on the mother."

BSF : "Jesus Christ, this is only Tuesday...that's what, three days?"

SM : "Yeah, and don't forget that yesterday was a holiday."

BSF: "Jesus, that's right—she could of tore it up the same night she picked it up."

SM: "Probably did...probably fucked it up putting it in the garage when she took it home that night."

BSF: "Son of a bitch, Ed, I been in the body and fender business for 25 years and I'll be goddamned if I can figure out how the mothers do it—and I've seen shit that no sane man would believe."

SM: "Don't knock it, Ernie, if it wasn't for broads and drunks, you wouldn't have no body shop at all."

- FADE -

or, Is Everybody Nuts But Me?

THE BANK JOB

SCENE

VTM's Uncle Fred's house in Ojai, CA, a few days after Christmas...Uncle Fred and VTM's Mother reminiscing about old days in Oklahoma.

CHARACTERS

- VTM's Mother (Vista)
- Uncle Fred (Vista's youngest brother)
- Aunt Patsy (Fred's wife)
- Loretta
- VTM

Vista: "Well, things were different when I went to school...we always behaved and did what we were told."

U. Fred: "Yeah..."

V: "And I don't mean just in class, either...we were always pretty well behaved at dances and other places too."

UF: "Yeah..."

V: "Fred, what was that Indian boy's name that was in my class there in Wewoka...Thoms or Thomas or something like that? I was thinking about him the other day."

UF: "Thompson, Hap Thompson."

V: "That's right! Hap Thompson...you know, he was ugly–for an Indian."

UF: "And dumb, too."

V: "He always had a crush on me—all the way through school he would always try to get a desk next to mine and everything."

UF: "Yeah, he wasn't too bright."

V: "I remember one time at the City Drug Store after school he asked me to go to a dance and I was so embarrassed I coulda' died."

UF: "That was old man Perkins' place—him and his partner. Old man Perkins was a widower, and did considerable playing around with some of the women there in town—nobody knew about it, though, but me and Walter and them."

V: "I don't know why I never wanted to go out with poor old Hap, except that he was so homely."

UF: "He married that Bunyard girl—Claude Bunyard's sister—and went to work at the Farmer's State Bank there in Wewoka."

V: "Didn't the Bunyard family own that bank?"

UF: "Yeah...I reckon that's how come Hap to go to work there right after the wedding."

V: "I remember those Bunyard boys—Claude had a twin brother—and they both got into trouble over something at the bank."

UF: "Embezzlement—they tucked 'em both away in McAlister."

V: "Did Hap get into trouble over that?"

UF: "Naw—Hap wasn't near smart enough to do any embezzlin'."

V: "You know, I remember that now...we always thought that the Bunyard family was really something, and it turned out that they were just a bunch of thieves."

A. Patsy: *(Seventy-five years old, and a little ringy)* "It sure is nice to get together and reminisce about the family, isn't it?...does anybody want some more coffee?"

- FADE -

GENERAL PAPER

SCENE

Loretta's apartment–Easter Sunday

CHARACTERS

- Loretta
- Loretta's mother (Opal)
- VTM (hung over)
- Chris (VTM's kid)

Loretta : "Mother, here are your presents for your birthday last week."

Opal : "Oh, are those for me?"

VTM : *(To self)* "A dialog will probably have to be written about this one."

L : "Go ahead and open them."

O : "My, the paper's so pretty I hate to tear it up."

L : "Yes, isn't it pretty?"

O : "It sure is pretty."

VTM : *(To self)* "Jesus, I hope we've established the thing about the paper."

L : "I bought several rolls of that paper down at Payless last week."

O : "Well, it sure is pretty."

L : "I never have any 'general' present paper–all I ever have is Christmas paper."

Chris : "Can I have another candy egg before dinner?"

VTM : "NO! For Christ's sake, you've had ten frigging eggs already."

C : "Aw...I never get to..."

VTM : "Cool it!"

L : "So, I thought–now's a good time to just stock up on 'general' paper...and then I'll have some when I need it."

O : "I should do that too, because all I ever have is Christmas paper."

VTM : *(To self)* "I wonder if a guy could get a drink down at Payless?"

L : "Well, Mother, go ahead and open your presents."

O : "I just hate to tear up this pretty paper...."

- FADE -

A Feast of Reason

LORETTA AND THE FUCK MOVIE

BACKGROUND

Loretta and VTM, having worked all day Saturday at Lockheed in preparation for a briefing of a high Department of Army official, adjourn to the Tao Tao bar for a few shooters. N (or, maybe N+1) shooters later (and a little screwed-up), decide to go across the street for a full-ride pizza and a sorely-needed liter of red wine.

CHARACTERS

- Loretta
- VTM
- Others

SCENE I

The Pizza Parlor, eating full-ride pizza and drinking sorely-needed wine.

Loretta: "Listen, Todd, let's go to an X-Rated Movie tonight."

VTM: "A Fuck Movie? Jesus, a few drinks and you become sex-crazed."

L: "No, really, Todd...you've never been to an X-Rated Movie and, at *your* age, you should be able to say that you've seen at least one."

VTM: "I'd sorta' like to keep my record clean in this respect."

L: "Jesus, don't be a *Goodie-Two-Shoes*."

or, Is Everybody Nuts But Me?

VTM: "*Goodie-Two-Shoes*, my ass...just because I don't want to see a Fuck Movie?"

L: "Aw, for Christ's sake . . . *etc., etc.*"

—SEVERAL ITERATIONS OF THIS CLASS CONVERSATION ENSUE—

SCENE II

The Fuck Movie, across the street from The Chinese Garden, and next door to Paul & Harvey's Saloon.

VTM: "Two, please."

Box Office Girl: "That'll be $11.00, please."

VTM: (*To self*) "Eleven dollars...Jesus, I saw <u>Gone With the Wind</u> for a quarter."

L: "Let's go in...you're going to love it."

VTM: "For eleven bucks, I better adore it."

Take seats in Fuck Movie—populated by three adenoidal youths and about 15 Old Farts with their hats in their laps (Doug Prins' line). On the screen are about 10 or 12 naked women and, maybe, half that number of naked guys—all intertwined on heavily carpeted floor in one gigantic group grope.

Sound Track: "Groan, sigh, moan..."

VTM: *(To self)* "Jesus Christ, I'm not going to be able to bear this for too long."

L: *(About eight minutes into Fuck Movie)* "I think I'm going to be sick."

VTM: "Wonderful."

L: "No, really, I feel sick at my...*heave, HEAVE, HEAVE!*"

...splash, splash, splash (sound of heave hitting concrete floor of Fuck Movie)

VTM: "Jesus."

L: "I'm going to the Ladies Room."

VTM: "It may be too late."

Loretta goes to Ladies Room, followed by VTM who waits in lobby, but keeps eye on Fuck Movie. By this time first feature has ended and second feature begins with N guys and broads lying around on floor, naked, etc., etc.

VTM: *(To self)* "Jesus, they must stamp these mothers out with a cookie cutter...Maybe only one Fuck Movie has ever been made, and they just change the title from time to time."

L: *(Sticking head out of Ladies Room)* "I've lost my glasses...will you go down and look where we were sitting?"

VTM: "Where, under that pile of heave?"

76

Goes down to seats, hands and knees, avoiding heave. Usher appears with flashlight.

Usher: "What did you lose?"

VTM: "Her glasses."

Usher: "Watch the heave."

VTM: "Thanks, Ace."

Does not find glasses, but finds Loretta's cigarette case and lighter–incredibly, free of heave...returns to lobby.

L: *(Sticking head out of Ladies Room)* "I found my glasses...they were on the back of the toilet."

VTM: "Let's get the hell out of here."

SCENE III

In the car–

L: "I'm sorry, Todd...I just don't know what happened. I was sitting there and, suddenly, I heaved."

VTM: "I sort of figured that out by myself."

L: "Well, you don't have to be pissed."

VTM: *(Who, at this juncture, has left about $26 at the Fuck Movie– $11 at the box office and approximately $15 on the floor, in the form of recycled pizza and sorely-needed red wine)* "I'm not pissed."

L: "Yes you are, and you shouldn't be because it's *your* fault anyway."

VTM: "What the hell do you mean 'It's my fault'?"

L: "Well, if *you* hadn't wanted to stay at the Tao so long, then I wouldn't have had so many screwdrivers—and it was *your* idea to have the pizza —and anyway, how about the time *you...etc.*"

VTM: "Bullshit, Loretta...It's *not* my fault, and I'm not pissed. I just want to go home and hose the puke off my shoes."

L: "I just don't know what happened...I was just sitting there when, suddenly, I...."

- FADE -

or, Is Everybody Nuts But Me?

EAR OF THE BEHOLDER

SCENE

VTM's cousin Wandell, and Wandie's good friend Curtis, standing on downtown street corner in Wewoka, Oklahoma (Pop. about 4,000). Both had recently recovered from surgery—Wandie on one ear, to alleviate a partial deafness, and Curtis on both eyes, to have cataracts removed.

CHARACTERS

- Wandell Billingsley
- Curtis Burch

Curtis: "Wandie, since I had my eyes operated on, I can see better than I ever could."

Wandie: "That right?"

Curtis: "Yeah, in fact I believe I can see better now than I could when I was a kid...for example—I know you can't see it—but there's an ant crawling up that lamp post over there on the corner."

Wandie: "No, I can't see it, Curtis, but I knew it was there...I could hear it walking."

-FADE-

A Feast of Reason

HE SOLD IT TO BOB STOKES FOR FIFTY DOLLARS

SCENE

In new Sooner-red GMC pickup (1500 Sierra SLE) traveling from Seminole, Oklahoma, to Wewoka (approximately 15 miles) following dinner at the Seminole Western Sizzler ("BBQ Bologna a Salad Bar Specialty").

CHARACTERS

- VTM
- VTM's Mother, Vista
- VTM's cousin, Weldon, a retired banker (Security State Bank, Wewoka), and the guy for whom the expression "He would give you the shirt off his back," was invented.

Weldon: "The thing I remember most about Seminole is the time Ol' Wandie♣ and Curtis Burch got all screwed up at the Trianon Ballroom♦ and Curtis fell back into one of those fake potted palms and couldn't get up. Ol' Curtis said that he wasn't even going to try to get up until somebody explained how come him to fall into the tree. Wandie said that he'd probably have to spend the rest of his life there then, because no sane person could ever explain how come him to fall into the tree."

VTM: *(To self)* "I'm not going to be able to bear too much of this."

W: "Ol' Curtis is bad sick now though with cancer, and it doesn't look too good."

♣ Wandell, Weldon's older brother, and maybe the nicest guy on earth.
♦ The Seminole, Oklahoma, Trianon Ballroom.

or, Is Everybody Nuts But Me?

Vista: "I always remembered that whole Burch family as being kind of sickly and puny and dying young."

W: "Well, now, Bertha lived to be 101, and would probably still be around if she hadn't fallen outa' that window."

VTM: *(To self)* "Jesus."

W: "And Lillian lived to be 92. Nobody ever knew how old Lillian really was, but I found her birth certificate after she died, when I had to open her safe deposit box down at the bank."

V: "Well, I do remember that the Burch family was pretty well off, and owned a lot of land and everything."

VTM: *(In a sickly, puny attempt to change the subject)* "Speaking of that, Weldon, what does land go for in this part of Oklahoma?"

W: "Well, that depends on a lot of factors such as the type of land, its location, the parcel size, and so on. In general, though, rural land around here will go for from around $100 to $300 an acre, depending on the variables. I bought 10 acres of good land not long ago that belonged to Ol' Buck Cartwright[*] before he died for $125 an acre."

VTM: "Where is the land?"

W: "Up in 32:10:8."

VTM: "Where?"

---

[*] See <u>Sam Houston and the Cherokees</u>

A Feast of Reason

W: "Up in 32:10:8–over there Southeast of Cromwell♣."

VTM: "Oh."

W: *(Pointing out windshield)* "See that crossroad up there? That's where C.L.♦ wrecked his last car. Ran right into the side of a brand new Pontiac and wiped out both cars. Fortunately, nobody was hurt bad. Well, he asked me to get rid of the car for him. It was a total wreck, but because the motor was still good, I was able to sell it to Ol' Bob Stokes for $50–made him take the whole car though. Well, a couple of days later, C.L. asked me if I was able to get anything for the car. I told him I got $50, and we were damned lucky to get that. 'Well,' he said, 'it had a half a tank of gas in it.'"

VTM: *(To self)* "Jesus Christ, if I could remember half of this shit, it would make the greatest dialog ever written. The trouble is, though, no one would ever believe it...especially in California, where people are a little square going in."

W: *(Pointing to house on outskirts of Wewoka)* "See that house over there? Ol' Sam Billups lived there for a while after he got out of the Retarded Home."

VTM: *(To self)* "I frigging can't bear much more of this."

W: "They had to let him go because he wasn't crazy...he was just a deaf-mute...couldn't hear or talk either."

VTM: *(To self)* "Jesus, you'd think that being a deaf-mute would be bad enough, let alone not being able to hear or talk, either."

♣ Oklahoma land measurement/location convention, i.e., Section 32, Range 10N, Township 8E.

♦ Uncle Clarence, Weldon's father.

or, Is Everybody Nuts But Me?

W. "Finally, Ol' Cecil Moore took him in on his dairy farm down in Sasakwa♣. Ol' Sam used to walk from Sasakwa to Wewoka, though most of the time somebody would come along and give him a lift in the back of their pickup."

VTM: *(To self)* "I'm going to jump out of the window."

W: "Ol' Sam couldn't talk, but he could make noises and, when you got to know him, you could figure out that he had different noises for different things. For example, his sound for 'door' was—

Weldon emits a kind of warbling growl

"...and if you knew Sam, you knew that meant 'door.'"

VTM: *(To self)* "Great fucking Christ!"

W: "He had a whole bunch of different sounds for different things, like—"

Produces six or eight different combinations of growls, grunts, half-barks, whistles, etc., with corresponding Billups-to-English translations.

VTM: *(To self)* "Please, God, tell me I'm not hearing this...I'm going to wake up in a minute and I'll be safe in my own bed at home."

♣ A small town about 20 miles south of Wewoka.

W: *(Dropping off VTM and VTM's Mother at Mother's place)* "Well, I enjoyed the dinner. I'll be over again around 9:00 in the morning. Remind me tomorrow, Todd, I've got a couple of really strange things I want to tell you about—like the time that Ol'...."

- FADE -

or, Is Everybody Nuts But Me?

A VOTE FOR CANONIZATION

SCENE

Long distance phone conversation in April, 1989, between VTM and the Texas Aggie (who has retired to South Carolina).

CHARACTERS

- VTM
- Lynn Jones

VTM: (*Ending conversation*) "Well, Lynn, that's about all the news from this end...oh yeah, one more thing—Loretta and I have been married for one year as of day before yesterday."

LJ: "One year already?"

VTM: "That's right."

LJ: "Has Loretta been sainted yet?"

- FADE -

A Feast of Reason

THE FIRE GIVER

SCENE

Sunday afternoon at home, VTM preparing to watch San Francisco 49ers–New Orleans Saints football game. Game is critical because 49ers and Saints are tied for lead in Western Division of NFC, with identical 7-2 records.

CHARACTERS

- VTM
- Loretta
- Bear (VTM's 3-legged girl dog)

Loretta: "It's a little chilly today; why don't you build a fire in the fireplace?"

VTM: "Loretta, I don't want to screw around with the fireplace, I want to watch the ball game."

L: "Well, it's kind of cool in here, and a fire would be nice."

VTM: "I realize that the temperature has plummeted to near 70°, but I believe that we can tough it out. If you're cold, turn on the furnace for a few minutes."

L: *(Coming up with the line no sane guy ever wants to hear from his wife)* "That's OK, you go ahead and watch the ball game, and *I'll* build the fire."

VTM: "For Christ's sake, Loretta, the fireplace has to be cleaned out and more wood brought in from the woodpile...just leave it alone."

OR, IS EVERYBODY NUTS BUT ME?

L: "No, you watch the game, and I'll take care of everything."

Loretta cleans out fireplace and, with Bear, makes N round trips to woodpile for kindling and logs. With the precise timing that is apparently genetic with women, manages to come between VTM and TV set on three critical 3rd down plays, and one run back of a pass interception. Prepares fire in fireplace with a combination of what appears to be several wadded up slick paper Sunday Supplement pages; about eight or ten small green tree branches; and three medium sized partially-seasoned eucalyptus logs (having a kindling temperature near that of asbestos).

L: "There, now, I'll just light this and we'll have a nice cheery Sunday afternoon fire."

VTM: *(To self)* "Bullshit, a direct napalm hit wouldn't ignite that mess."

Loretta lights colored paper in several places; paper flares up briefly, goes out, and flame is replaced by a single small tendril of vertically-rising smoke.

VTM: *(To self)* "Jesus, I feel like a Hiroshima survivor."
(To Loretta) "I hope Bear wasn't badly burned."

L: "I just don't know what happened...I've built dozens of fires before...Why, when I was a little girl and we lived out in the woods in Oregon..."

—Lays out about a paragraph and a half of Oregonian woodcraft lore—

VTM: "Goddammit, Loretta, go sit down and I'll build the damn fire...then I'd like to watch the frigging game."

L: "No, I'll fix it...all it needs is more paper."

VTM: "Go sit over there where I can watch you, and I'll take care of it."

VTM opens fire screen, removes scorched remains of <u>Parade</u> magazine, several wadded up grocery store coupon pages, eight or ten unscathed small green tree branches, and three eucalyptus logs. Bundles up branches to give to Loretta–

VTM: "Here's your kindling...put these branches over on the sofa...I'd hate to see anything bad happen to them."

L: "Jesus, you're a smartass."

VTM prepares fire with regular newspaper, dry kindling sticks, several old 2 x 4's, three eucalyptus logs, and several squirts of charcoal starter–

L: *(Watching, with hands on hips)* "Well, I don't know why you think that's going to be any better...that's exactly what *I* did."

VTM: "Yeah"

VTM tosses in match which, within 20 seconds, produces a standard Mark I fireplace fire–

VTM: "There's your goddamned fire, Loretta...now I would like to be allowed to salvage what's left of this frigging football game."

L: "I don't know what's the matter with you...all I wanted was a nice little fire on Sunday afternoon...Jesus, men are insensitive...I simply never have been able to understand why men always...."

- FADE -

TEE OFF TIME

SCENE

VTM and VTM's only girl cousin, Nancy*, driving down freeway to San Jose Airport.

CHARACTERS

- Nancy
- VTM
- Joe, Nancy's husband, (not present)

N: "You know, Joe just turned 70 and he's cut way back on his law practice. In fact, he recently gave up his Law Office and converted one of the bedrooms at home into an office."

VTM: "Yeah, he told me that."

N: Sooner or later, he's going to have to quit altogether, and I just don't know how he's going to handle it."

VTM: "Why is that?"

N: "Well, for one thing, I just don't know what he's going to do with his time—Joe's never had any hobbies or anything. His only interest has always been his work."

VTM: "Yeah, and at 70, he's too old to jerk off."

---

* AKA "Magnolia, the Flower of Southern Womanhood."

N: "Yes, that's right, but then Joe never has shown any interest in golf."

- FADE -

A Feast of Reason

GREAT MOMENTS IN AMERICAN LITERATURE

SCENE

VTM's boat, docked at Perry's Boat Harbor on Mokelumne River in California River Delta. Bill Higdon and Loretta are conversing on cockpit deck; VTM is below cleaning up main cabin, but can overhear conversation.

CHARACTERS

- Bill Higdon (3/4 in the bag)
- Loretta (also with the program)
- VTM (a picture of moderation and restraint)
- Marge (Higdon's wife—not present)

BH: "I'm writing a book on my computer...it's about my life—the places I've been, people I've known, things I've seen and done, and stuff like that."

VTM: *(To self)* "I believe that's called an autobiography."

L: "How neat. I'm writing a book on my computer too, only it's fiction...a mystery story, actually."

BH: "Well, mine's not for publication—it's more just for family members, but Marge has been reading it, and she thinks that other people would also find it interesting."

L: "Well, that may be; you've led an interesting life."

BH: "I don't know how anybody would be interested in my life, but Marge thinks so. Of course, being my wife, she's bound to be a little biased. I should probably have somebody else look at it."

or, Is Everybody Nuts But Me?

L: "I'd be glad to look at it, Bill, but I've got to warn you that I'm the World's toughest critic."

BH: "I'd like for you to look at it...I've got about six chapters done...It's just that I don't know why anybody would be interested in my life."

L: "Well, I'll read it, but don't get your feelings hurt, because I'm the World's toughest critic."

VTM: *(To self)* "They're doing a variation on 'I was there, but I never seen you.'" *(Richard Bissel, 7 1/2 Cents - ED.)*

BH: "I'd sure like for you to read it, it's just that I don't understand why anybody would be interested in my life."

L: "Well, I'll read it, but don't be offended because I'm the World's toughest critic.

VTM: *(To self)* "It may be that this thermodynamic system is approaching equilibrium."

L: Incidentally, Bill, when I get my stuff cleaned up a little, you might be interested in reading it."

BH: "No, I don't read fiction–it puts me to sleep."

L: "Well, OK–I just thought that you might be interested."

BH: "No, I don't read fiction...in fact, almost everything I read puts me to sleep...except for the Scientific American."

VTM: *(To self)* "I can see how that would keep a guy right on the edge of his chair."

L: "Well, OK, but I'll still read yours, but don't be offended, because...etc."

BH: "I'd sure like for you to, but I just don't understand why...etc."

- FADE -

OR, IS EVERYBODY NUTS BUT ME?

IF I LIVED HERE, I'D BE HOME NOW

SCENE

After a hard Sunday of watching football on TV, VTM and Loretta go to bed early. Around 9:00 PM, VTM is awakened by insistent ringing of telephone in other room.

CHARACTERS

- VTM
- Loretta
- Chris—VTM's son (around 24 years old at this juncture)

VTM: *(Answering phone while still half asleep)* "Hello."

Chris: "Dad, in about 15 minutes there's going to be a lunar eclipse...I wanted to let you know so you wouldn't miss it."

VTM: "Jesus, Chris, it's been raining for two days now, and the sky's completely overcast—what do you think you're going to be able to see?"

C: "Well, if the sky clears up in the next 15 minutes, there's going to be this neat lunar eclipse."

VTM: "Yeah, well, OK, Chris, thanks for letting me know."

VTM hangs up phone, returns to bedroom, sits on edge of bed, and attempts to evaluate Fate's latest application of the shaft—

VTM: *(To self)* "As I understand this thing, if:

1. I get dressed and go outside, and

2. The clouds clear at the proper time and place in the sky, then

3. I won't be able to see the moon.

Goddammit, I already can't see the moon...and when I was fast asleep in my own bed, I *really* couldn't see the frigging moon...Jesus...I wonder if a guy can still buy an assault rifle without the five-day wait..."

Loretta: "What's the matter with you? Jesus, I wish you'd stop mumbling and turn out the light so we can get some sleep...*I* have to get up early in the morning, and..."

- FADE -

or, Is Everybody Nuts But Me?

WHAT ELSE?

SCENE

Uncle Fred's house in Ojai, CA, discussing family, the "old days" in Oklahoma, etc.

CHARACTERS

- Uncle Fred
- Aunt Patsy
- Vista, VTM's Mother
- VTM

Vista: "Fred, remember when we were kids and lived down on the farm near Stuart, we had an old one-eyed hound dog…I've been thinking about him lately, and, for the life of me, I can't remember his name."

U. Fred: "Good-Eye."

- FADE -

A Feast of Reason

ARISTOTELIAN LOGIC

SCENE

VTM and VTM's Mother, Vista, discussing family history, kinfolks, how kids get named, etc.

CHARACTERS

- VTM
- Vista, VTM's Mother

VTM: "You know, I've always liked the name Todd—it's an old family name, it's short, and fairly uncommon—or, at least, used to be. On the other hand, I hate the name Victor—and that's why I've never used it."

Vista: "Why, Todd, you always loved your Uncle Victor."

-FADE-

or, Is Everybody Nuts But Me?

CULTURE SHOCK

SCENE I

VTM and Loretta on plane from Oklahoma City to DFW, returning to California following an Oklahoma–Kansas football game at Norman, OK. (KU 38, OU 17). VTM overhears conversation between two guys seated immediately aft.

CHARACTERS

- Loretta
- VTM
- 1st Guy
- 2nd Guy

1st Guy: "Jesus, what a lousy game. OU looked real bad after the 1st quarter."

2nd Guy: "That's sure a fact. I'll tell you one thing–if Schnellenberger is going to run that pro-style offense at Oklahoma, the first thing he better do is get a quarterback who can pass."

1st G: "That's for sure–neither one of those two kids he's got can hit the side of the Student Union."

2nd G: "Yeah, 5 for 20 with two interceptions...Jesus Christ."

1st G: "And another thing...that defensive backfield ain't for shit...Did you see how far the Oklahoma corners were playing off the KU wide receivers?"

2nd G: "Yeah, all they did was lay back in that damn two-deep zone and let Kansas eat 'em up."

A Feast of Reason

1st G: "Yeah, especially when Kansas picked up the blitz...I don't know why Schnellenberger doesn't...etc., etc."

SCENE II

Having changed planes at DFW, VTM and Loretta are headed for San Jose. VTM overhears conversation between two guys seated immediately aft.

CHARACTERS

- Loretta
- VTM
- 3rd Guy
- 4th Guy

3rd Guy: "Well, I work for 3Com, but my real interest is bicycles."

4th Guy: "Is that right? I do a lot of riding myself—I have a mountain bike."

3rd G: "I build my own bikes—in fact, I just finished one. It's a real killer going down hill, but going uphill, it sucks."

4th G: "You mean you build them from scratch?"

3rd G: "Yeah, I even make my own cranks. I'm building a bike now for a friend of mine. He weighs 230 pounds, which presents some problems—for one thing, I had to hand-select each tube that will go into the frame."

4th G: "Well, I never tried to build a bike, but I sure enjoy riding. Once a week, several of us get together and ride from Milpitas

or, Is Everybody Nuts But Me?

          to Mountain View. It's a good ride, but sometimes the wind off the bay is simply devastating."

3rd G: "Yeah, I ride with a group, too. Every day at 3Com, we ride for an hour at lunch...and on weekends, we...etc., etc."

Loretta: "You can sure tell when you're back in California, can't you?"

VTM: "Yeah,"...*(SIGH)*..."Jesus."

- FADE -

A Feast of Reason

THE GREAT CONE HETERODOX

SCENE

VTM and Loretta having just finished eating three pre-packaged frozen ice cream cones (Loretta–one cone; VTM–two cones).

CHARACTERS

- VTM
- Loretta

VTM: "These sugar cones are usually firm and crisp, but both of mine were soggy and limp.

Loretta: "Well, mine was just right."

VTM: "Not only that, the tip of my first cone broke off, allowing the ice cream to drip all over the front of my shirt."

L: "Well, my cone was just right."

VTM: "The second cone was even worse...it had the consistency of wet wallpaper."

L: "Well, my cone was just right."

VTM: *(Growing semi-testy)* "Notwithstanding that, Loretta, my cones were limp and soggy.

L: "Well, I don't see why your cones were soggy and mine was crisp—when they all came out of the same package."

VTM: *(To self)* "I'll be goddamned if I'm going to discuss non-linear heat transfer with her." *(To Loretta)* "I don't give a shit about

OR, IS EVERYBODY NUTS BUT ME?

your cone, Loretta. My cones were, in indisputable fact, limp and soggy."

L: "Well, I still don't see why your cones were soggy and mine was nice and crisp, when they all came out...etc."

VTM: "Loretta, for Christ's sake...please..."

- FADE -

A Feast of Reason

or, Is Everybody Nuts But Me?

A PARALLEL UNIVERSE

Obviously, some really great conversations occur in situations other than at work or among family members. Offered here are some real dandies that were overheard—or participated in—by the writer in various public places, i.e., saloons, restaurants, and, in one case, during a hospital incarceration. While the reader's credulity may be tested, fidelity prevails—in fact, these dialogs are not even semi-stretchers.

A PARALLEL UNIVERSE

Falconcrest	107
A Matter of Pronunciation	109
Cause and Effect	110
You Don't Have To Buy Nothing To Win	111
The Athenaeum Alumni Association	114
The Vicissitudes of Time	117
The Evening News	118
A Matter of Perception	120
It's Them Russians	121
Points of View	125
Adventures in Beer	127
The Essential Issue	129
Only in Ohio	131
The Death Certificate	136
Maybe It's Only An Expression	140
The All-Conference Greeter	141
A Fool And His Money	144
Relative Time	145
The Care Givers	146

or, Is Everybody Nuts But Me?

FALCONCREST

SCENE

Hotel bar in St. Louis, Missouri

CHARACTERS

- Bartender (a young guy)
- Young female customer
- VTM
- John Strain

YF: "Oh, is that 'Falconcrest' on the TV? —Far out!"

BT: "I think so."

YF: "How did they get out of that fire?"

BT: "I don't know."

YF: "Was her face burned?"

BT: "I don't know...I have to work during the evening."

YF: "Do you think Greg and Ginny will ever get back together again?"

BT: "Maybe."

YF: "Is Greg walking yet?"

BT: "I missed that part, but I hope so because I think Greg is a really nice guy."

YF: "So do I—He looks like Donny Osmond."

J. Strain: *(Who has entered bar unseen by VTM.)* "What the hell are you doing watching a soap opera?"

VTM: "Fuck you."

- FADE -

or, Is Everybody Nuts But Me?

A MATTER OF PRONUNCIATION

SCENE

A saloon in Nogales, Mexico (*Part 1*)...John Strain nostalgically recalling previous experiences in Mexico.

CHARACTERS

- John Strain (half in the bag)
- VTM (likewise)

JS: "I remember one time down in the state of Chihuahua, I had a chance to visit Poncho *Vee-yah's Vil-la*.

VTM: "Are you sure that it's not Poncho *Vil-la's Vee-yah*?"

JS: "Fuck you."

- FADE -

A Feast of Reason

CAUSE AND EFFECT

SCENE

A saloon in Nogales, Mexico (*Part 2*)

CHARACTERS

- John Strain
- Mexican bartender
- VTM

> *Mexican bartender takes a brief break during which he avails himself of a couple of tacos and a large bottle of Dr. Pepper.*

VTM: *(To bartender)* "You probably don't know this, buddy, but drinking Dr. Pepper will make you crazy."

MB: "It cannot be my friend, for you see, I am already crazy."

-FADE-

or, Is Everybody Nuts But Me?

YOU DON'T HAVE TO BUY NOTHING TO WIN

SCENE

Tombstone, Arizona; Top O' the Hill Cafe (Hickory Smoked Bar-B-Q, Sizzlin' Steaks, Chili). Around 8:30 AM, with customers seated around horseshoe-shaped counter.

CHARACTERS

- Three Old Boys (OB) in Levis, boots, and cowboy hats
- Young Female (YF)
- Middle Aged Female (MAF)
- Waitress
- VTM

1st OB : "I got a letter in the mail Saturday from some outfit running a contest with $100,000 worth of prizes. They also had some stuff a man could buy, but said you didn't have to buy nothing to be eligible for the prizes...just had to return the card with your name on it."

2nd OB : "I got a picture of you winning a prize if you don't buy nothing."

3rd OB : "Ain't that the truth."

YF: "No, I seen a program on TV called '20-20' where they said it was the law that they had to draw your name whether you bought nothing or not."

W'tress: "I think I seen that too."

MAF:	*(Entering cafe)* "Well, I just come from the Post Office and they got a new sign that says no dogs allowed except seeing-eye dogs and I never seen a dog that could read."
2nd OB:	"Hello, Darlene. Well, they may have to draw your name, but that don't mean they have to give you a prize."
3rd OB:	"Yeah, I reckon your card goes right in the wastepaper basket."
YF:	"No, they said on '20-20' that..."
MAF:	"Did you guys hear the one about the pig with the wooden leg?"
1st OB:	"You told us that one last week, Darlene."
MAF:	"How about the one about the three niggers in the space ship?"
VTM:	*(To self)* "Jesus, it's got to be either a variation on 'The Jig is Up,' or it's got something to do with Moon Pies."
1st OB:	"Now, I don't believe you told us that one."
MAF:	"Well, there was these three niggers in this space ship and..."

—*4th Old Boy enters Cafe*—

3 OB's:	"By God, here comes trouble." "Ain't that the truth." "By God, it's old Grover."

or, Is Everybody Nuts But Me?

Old
Grover: "Ain't you three got nothin' to do but sit around drinking coffee all morning?—Hello Darlene."

MAF: "Hello Grover...So the first nigger says..."

OG: "I got a letter in the mail Saturday on this contest where they said you don't have to buy nothing to win a prize."

VTM: *(To self)* "Mother of God, it's *'Our Town'*."

YF: "That's right, on '20-20' they said that you don't..."

- FADE -

THE ATHENAEUM ALUMNI ASSOCIATION

SCENE

Sutter's Place, a combination 24-hr card room (5-Card Stud, Lo-Ball, and Pan), 6 AM saloon, and greasy-spoon cafe, located on the outskirts of Alviso, CA, queen city of the South Bay sloughs and home of the Greater San Jose Municipal Sewage Disposal Facility. In addition to VTM, Sutter's is frequented largely by Hispanic and Asian card players, short haul truck drivers, motorcycle riders and, what Paul Skelton once described as 'anvil makers.'

CHARACTERS

- Marv Martin♣, one of the nicest and smartest guys around, but sometimes a little square around the edges.
- Sixty-year-old female bartender (FB) with a missing front tooth and a profile like a broken plank.
- Mexican patron at end of bar, getting well on peppermint schnapps with a beer back.
- A drunk seated about five stools away, passed out with head on bar.
- VTM

Marv: "You know, this place reminds me a lot of London."

VTM: "I'm kind of curious as to how you put that one together, Marv."

Marv: "Well, the place has atmosphere, like a lot of the old pubs in London."

♣ See CAST OF PRINCIPAL CHARACTERS

VTM: "They probably don't play a whole lot of Pan in London, though."

Marv: *(Addressing Female Bartender, after ordering drinks)* "I go to London quite often, and I always stay at the Athenaeum; do you know the Athenaeum?"

FB: "Well, no, I don't believe I do."

VTM: *(To self)* "Jesus, if that old broad has ever been out of Santa Clara County, it would only have been to attend the Roller Derby up at the Cow Palace."

Marv: "Oh, you must know it...it's in Piccadilly, just down from the Wellington Arch, and directly across from Green Park."

FB: "Well, no, I..."

Marv: "It's very conveniently located for shopping—both the Burlington Arcade and Harrods are within easy walking distance."

—*Schnapps & beer Mexican favors Marv with a glance of thinly-veiled disbelief*—

VTM: *(In a semi-whisper)* "Jesus, Marv, you're not exactly talking to the Stanford sailboat set, here."

Marv: *(Ignoring VTM)* "It's also near many of the good theaters and, as you probably know, the London stage productions are superb."

VTM: *(To self)* "Mother of Christ."

A Feast of Reason

—Passed-out drunk comes to life, raises head from bar, and blinks owlishly several times in an apparent effort to come to grips with what has transpired during his sabbatical—

Marv: *(Obviously encouraged by the one-third increase in the size of his Alviso-based audience)* "There are also many outstanding restaurants in the vicinity, particularly if you like genuine old-world Italian food or East Indian cuisine...the curries are outstanding, with authentic Chutney, and served with..."

VTM: *(Interrupting)* "It's getting late, Marv, we'd better get you to the airport so you don't miss your plane back to L.A."

Marv: *(With bit now firmly between teeth)* "Oh no, there's plenty of time...now the Athenaeum is a little on the expensive side, but I always say that if you're going to spend the money to get to Britain, then you might as well enjoy the...."

- FADE -

or, Is Everybody Nuts But Me?

THE VICISSITUDES OF TIME

SCENE

Otto's Garden Room, an honest-to-God honky tonk frequented by VTM, motorcycle riders, construction workers, and anvil makers. VTM is seated in customary seat at end of bar where he overhears conversation between two older guys a couple of stools away.

CHARACTERS

- VTM
- Older Guy 1 (OG-1)
- Older Guy 2 (OG-2)

OG-1: "Ed, I'll tell you one thing— I've had a bellyful of this getting old shit. It seems like every goddamned day, I wake up with some new kind of ache or twinge."

OG-2: "Yeah, and that ain't the worst of it—a man's sex life begins to go to hell, too."

OG-1: "By God, that's a fact. I ain't been laid in so long my Viagra pills have come out from under warranty."

-FADE-

A Feast of Reason

THE EVENING NEWS

SCENE

Tao Tao bar around 5:30 PM on a weekday evening.

CHARACTERS

- Chinese Bartenders - Kingman and Moi*
- VTM

K: *(Reaching for TV in corner of back bar)* "Would you like to hear News, Mr. Miller?"

VTM: "I don't care, Kingman—whatever you guys want——It really doesn't make any difference, though, because the after-work ladies will be hitting here pretty soon, and we won't be able to hear anything over the noise of the blenders."

M: *(Being familiar with—and delighting in—VTM's often voiced intolerance of the triviality of the local TV News)* "Yes...turn on, turn on!!—he like News."

—Kingman turns on TV in time for first item of compelling interest. Diane Feinstein, Mayor of San Francisco, has proposed that the much-discussed new stadium (to replace Candlestick Park) be located on a parcel of land adjacent to San Francisco International Airport.

VTM : *(With microsecond response)* "Why, that stupid goddamned broad...why doesn't someone knock her in the fucking head? A ballpark in that location would have all the drawbacks of Candlestick—wind, cold, fog—but would be even harder to get

---
*See CAST OF PRINCIPAL CHARACTERS

in and out of, with all the traffic around SFO. It might be convenient for some guy flying in from Chicago to see a game, but it sure as hell wouldn't be for anyone who lives in the Bay Area. Jesus, what a stupid idea...that's dumb even for a San Francisco politician." *(Lapses into muttered sexist invective.)*

—The next news item is an interview with a guy in the East Bay whose claim to fame is that he rides a bicycle 50 miles every day to work and back (and, therefore, doesn't pollute the atmosphere like the rest of us ecological criminals). The guy is a caricature of your standard Mark I Bay Area Liberal (skinny, with beard, wild hair, and dime-size granny glasses; denim pants with one torn knee, etc., In general, projects the appearance of a walking dust mop).

VTM: *(Instant towering rage)* "Why that simple son-of-a-bitch. Jesus, I've had a bellyful of those assholes and their silly-ass bicycle suits and wimpy helmets with the cute little mirror on the side. Did you ever notice, Kingman, that the only time you ever see those Schwinn Freaks is either on a narrow mountain road with no shoulders, or on a main traffic artery during rush hour, where they can really fuck things up. Shit, five or six of those idiots, strategically placed during rush hour, would bring the entire Bay Area to its knees. We ought to get all those fuckheads together in one place and napalm 'em—though a case might be made for individual strangulation." *(Again lapses into muttering, while visibly attempting to regain self-control, and reduce heart rate).*

M: *(Who has appeared from opposite end of bar)* "Must look at bright side, Todd. Many people will ride bicycle to new stadium..."

- FADE -

A Feast of Reason

A MATTER OF PERCEPTION

SCENE

A November Saturday afternoon at VTM's house, watching an Oklahoma/Nebraska football game on TV.

CHARACTERS

- David Hemmes (Heems). A known software guy as well as a product of the Southern California beach culture. Thus, Heem's idea of sports is centered largely on Frisbee throwing, bicycle riding, and motorcycle racing.
- VTM

DH: "Why do the Nebraska guys have "Z's" on the side of their helmets?"

VTM: "Because they're bending over in the huddle, Heems."

- FADE -

or, Is Everybody Nuts But Me?

IT'S THEM RUSSIANS

SCENE

The "Village Gent," a beer bar in Cupertino, CA, with two pool tables and a blackboard menu offering the following microwave fare:

- Beans & Franks $2.50
- Spaghetti & Meatballs 2.50
- Hot dog (1/4 lb)   1.75
- Chile   1.50
- Cream of Mushroom soup 1.50

It is around 11:00 AM when VTM appears for a restorative beer.

CHARACTERS

- An old boy, obviously from Arkansas, who is a dead ringer for Marvelous Marv Throneberry, the N.Y. Mets original First Baseman
- A young guy from San Diego (but originally from Ohio)
- Bartender
- VTM

Marvelous
Marv: "You all been readin' about them captives?"

San Diego
Kid: "Yes, and what about that Air India plane that got bombed?"

MM: "Yeah, all this weird shit's goin' on, and the United States don't seem to be able to do nothin' about it."

SDK: "Yes, and remember that Korean airliner that the Russians shot down?"

MM: "You know, them Russians is the *real* assholes in all of this crap."

SDK: "That's a fact!...and, yet, we have people in this country who have nothing better to do than to demonstrate and protest against everything our government tries to do–chaining themselves to fences, and things like that."

MM: "You don't see nobody chaining themselves to no Russian fences, and they're the *real* assholes behind all this crap."

VTM: *(To bartender)* "May I have a draft beer, while all this foreign policy is being developed?"

SDK: "Yes, the Russians are little better than the Germans were in World War II...killing all the Jews and Gypsies and Catholics."

MM: "And queers...they done it to everybody."

SDK: "Yes, well the world is just as crazy today–I guess it's just a matter of time until some nut presses the button and blows the whole world off the face of the earth *(sic)*."

VTM: *(To self)* "The guy's a phrase maker."

MM: "Well I ain't goin' to worry about it no more, nohow...I'm about ready to go on back to Arkansas."

VTM: *(To self)* "I frigging knew it!"

B'tender: *(Looking out front door)* "Looks like it's heating up out there...going to be another hot one today."

MM: "I done some work in L.A. recently, and it's sure hot down there—and all that smog on top of it."

SDK: "Yes, but at least they don't have the high humidity like in Ohio."

MM: "Buddy, you ain't seen no humidity like they got in Arkansas."

SDK: "Yes, well one thing about L.A. is that the humidity is fairly low."

MM: "That may be, but as far as I'm concerned, they can give that whole fuckin' place back to the Mexicans."

SDK: "San Diego is really *the* nice place down there...the climate is good, there are all kinds of things to do, but, still, it's not L.A."

VTM: *(To self)* "Weigh that, friends."

Loretta: *(Who has appeared out of nowhere)* "I thought you were going to meet me in the Burger Pit, not in the bar *behind* the Burger Pit."

VTM: "I can't bear the Burger Pit anymore—it's full of broads and wimps, and dumbass conversation...how did you find me anyway?"

L: "Well, when you weren't in the Burger Pit, it was just a matter of finding the closest saloon."

VTM: "I've got to change the whole defensive backfield scheme...I've got to do a better job of disguising the zone."

MM: "My radiator hose give out this morning and the car ain't got but 55,000 miles on her."

VTM: "This place is a lot better than the Burger Pit, anyway. For example, based on the information I've gathered here this morning, I've begun to have second thoughts about my career. The only problem is that I can't decide whether I want to enter the Foreign Service, or become a TV Meteorologist."

L: "Jesus, how long have you been in here, anyway? I can't turn my back on you anymore without you...etc."

-FADE-

or, Is Everybody Nuts But Me?

POINTS OF VIEW

SCENE

Chuck Franklin's house, mid 1980's.

CHARACTERS

- Chuck Franklin, an electronics, computer, autopilot guy (all weird), and, in the 1970s, probably the only hippie in California who wore designer jeans and drove a Cadillac Sedan de Ville.
- Chuck's wife, Margaret, a Palo Alto High School Spanish teacher

M: "I think it's just awful about the Moroccan Army firing on those people trying to cross their border."

C: "Jesus, Margaret, they were trying to take over a section of the country. The Moroccan government has every right to prevent that."

M: "Well, there's plenty of land there for everyone; I think they should have just let them have it."

C: "Margaret, what if 100,000 Mexicans suddenly decided to cross into California and take over some of our land?"

M: "Well, we have plenty of land...we could share some with them."

C: "Yes, but Margaret, what if they all wanted to come to Palo Alto and teach Spanish?"

-FADE-

or, Is Everybody Nuts But Me?

ADVENTURES IN BEER

SCENE

Black Watch saloon in downtown Los Gatos, CA–around 11:30 AM on a Thursday. VTM enters saloon, assumes customary seat at short end of bar, and orders a hit. A few minutes later two guys enter and take stools near VTM.

CHARACTERS

- Guy 1
- Guy 2
- Bartender (BT)
- VTM

Guy 1: *(to BT)* "I'll have a screwdriver; *(to Guy 2)* "What'll you have?"

Guy 2: "I'll have a Bud Lite."

—*BT brings drinks*—

Guy 2: "Why this is a Miller Lite–I ordered a Bud Lite."

BT: "I'm sorry...I thought you ordered a Miller's. Let me take it back, and I'll bring you a Bud."

Guy 2: "No, that's OK, I'll drink this."

BT: "No, it was my mistake–I'll be glad to bring you a Bud."

Guy 2: "No, that's OK, I'll try Miller's for a change."

—*BT apologizes again and leaves*—

Guy 1: "*I* thought you ordered a Bud Lite."

Guy 2: "I thought I did too, but when he brought the bottle I glanced at the label and thought 'hell, what have they done, changed the label again?' Ha, ha, ha."

Guy 1: "Ha, ha, ha, ha."

VTM: *(To self)* "Mother of God."

Guy 2: "This same thing happened to me one time in Reno...I ordered a–I think it was a Coors–and the guy brought something else–I can't remember what it was, but I know it wasn't a Coors."

Guy 1: "Yeah, that happens to me every once in a while, too...you can count on it, like death and taxes–Ha, ha."

Guy 2: "I guess that's right–Ha, ha, ha."

VTM: *(To self)* "From time to time, it becomes clear to me why a guy, armed with an automatic assault rifle, will suddenly...."

- FADE -

or, Is Everybody Nuts But Me?

THE ESSENTIAL ISSUE

SCENE

Almost empty bar of Garden City Card Room & Restaurant (San Jose, CA), around 11:00 AM.

CHARACTERS

- Impassive Oriental bartender
- Young Guy, a Garden City employee, who has just returned from a three-week vacation abroad.
- VTM

Young Guy: *(Entering bar from kitchen and addressing bartender)* "Hello, Winston. I just this minute got back from three weeks in Britain, Scotland, and Ireland. It was the most *incredible* experience of my *entire* life."

B'tender: *(Acknowledges kid's presence with a nod, while busy wiping glasses with bar towel.)*

YG: "That's the most beautiful area I've ever seen in my *entire* life. The green in Ireland is so *vivid* as to be almost *unreal*."

—*Bartender continues to dry glasses while looking at kid with zero expression*—

YG: "And Scotland...Oh, my God!! The sheer lonely, empty *grandeur* of the moors."

—*Bartender continues to wipe glasses while exhibiting the facial mobility of a skillet bottom*—

VTM: *(To self)* "Jesus, I know that guy can talk and hear. He said 'Good Morning' to me and brought me the right beer."

YG: "And the Lake Country in England..." *(continues emotional descriptions of landscape, saying 'like,' 'basically,' 'totally,' 'relate to,' and 'unreal' a lot, interspersed with many 'ums,', the way young guys talk)*

—Kid finally runs down, and about five seconds of silence elapse—

B T: "So, did you get any pussy?"

- FADE -

or, Is Everybody Nuts But Me?

ONLY IN OHIO

BACKGROUND

VTM in Dayton, Ohio, to attend annual unmanned vehicle symposium (AUVS-90). After an incredibly interesting morning of technical papers, flees from formal luncheon for attendees (with speaker, humorous anecdotes, etc.); sets out on foot in downtown Dayton in search of a saloon; finds King Cole restaurant.

SCENE

Bar of King Cole restaurant on ground floor of Kettering Tower (2nd and Main Streets) in downtown Dayton, Ohio.

CHARACTERS

- Bartender (John)
- Waitress (Cathy)
- Retired local doctor (Doc)
- Several local businessmen
- VTM

VTM: *(To self, entering bar)* "Jesus, this is a nice cool, dark, quiet place...outstanding for Dayton." *Notes dark wood paneling, large gilt-framed pictures (two French Impressionist, one Dutch Master, one John Constable-type landscape, and one Greek temple, by moonlight–school unknown). Assumes seat at bar.*

B'tender: "Yessir, what can I get for you?...Why, hello Doc, how are you?" (*Interrupts proceedings to address 200 year old man approaching bar.*)

Doc: "Well John, Earl McManus finally died of cancer Monday-week."

BT: "I heard that only yesterday. Sure was a shame."

D: "Sure was...hell, he was only 72, but he'd been losing weight and had been in a lot of pain for the last couple of months."

BT: "Well, maybe it was a blessing in disguise, etc., etc." *(Several repetitions of this and similar expressions of sorrow)...Doc leaves.*

VTM: *(To bartender)* "A dry martini up with a twist would be good."

BT: "Yessir." *Goes to other end of bar where three local businessmen—obviously regulars—are having drinks.*

1st BM: *(NOTE: In this case, "BM" stands for businessman)* "Were you and Doc talking about old Earl McManus dyin'?"

BT: "Yes, and it sure was a shame, etc., etc."

2nd BM: "Well, at least old Earl died of bein' sick. I heard the other day that some old boy got shot through the side of the head over at the Rest Home."

VTM: *(To self)* "Jesus Christ...why do I always end up hearing this kind of stuff?"

3rd BM: "Yeah, I heard about that. Hell, you'd figure a man would be safe in the *Home*."

1st BM: "Yeah. Only in America, right?"

3rd BM: "Right. Only in America."

or, Is Everybody Nuts But Me?

BT: "Only in America."

VTM: *(To self)* "Mother of Christ."

1st BM: "Well, the little woman and I are going back to Florida on vacation again this year."

3rd BM: "Where in Florida?"

1st BM: "Delray Beach. Delray Beach is the cleanest beach in the state of Florida."

2nd BM: "I always heard Miami Beach was good."

1st BM: "Hell no. It's full of loud New York Jews, and dirty besides. Delray Beach is the cleanest beach in the state of Florida."

3rd BM: "Well, it ought to be. I heard they spent 12 million dollars cleanin' it up."

VTM: "John, give me another mart, but make it a double this time."

2nd BM: "In the old days, my mother and her second husband *(Herbert, it later emerged)* use' to go to Louisville, KY, every year, and stay at the same hotel, every time. One time, there was a black dog with white feet in the alley just below their window who would knock over the garbage cans to get food. He would show up every morning at the same time. My mother named him 'Boots-the-Wanderer.' Later, when they got a dog of their own, they named him 'Boots-the-Wanderer' after that dog, because he was so smart...only they just called him 'Bootsie.'"

BT: "What was the first dog's name?"

2nd BM: "'Boots-the-Wanderer,' because of his feet and the garbage cans and coming around at the same time every day. My mother named him that."

3rd BM: "I remember your mother—she could charm the eyeballs out of a rattlesnake."

2nd BM: "Boy, that's sure the truth—but she's gone now."

VTM: *(To self)* "This bar shouldn't be on the ground floor—it should be on the top floor of the tower, with an open window that a guy could jump out of."

W'tress: *(Who has appeared at service bar)* "Two glasses of Cab-er-nay wine, John. My God, I don't know how people can stand to drink warm wine."

BT: "It's not warm, Cathy, it's served at room temperature."

W: "Well, if I was to drink it, I'd put ice in it."

Departs with tray of wine.

3rd BM: "We use' to go to Florida on vacation, but the last few years we been goin' to South America. Last year, we went to Ur-a-gway."

1st BM: "We been to Para-gway, but never to Ur-a-gway."

3rd BM: "Well, you'd like Ur-a-gway better."

2nd BM: "I been to Bolivia and once to Lima *(as in bean)* Peru, but never to Ur-a-gway."

3rd BM: "Well, you'd like Ur-a-gway better."

VTM: *(To self)* "Jesus, I've fallen in with the Dayton, Ohio, Jet Set." *(To bartender)* "John, I believe I'll have one more." *(To waitress)* "Cathy, I'd like the T-Bone medium rare and a glass of that Cab-er-nay...only, don't put any ice in the Cab-er-nay."

W: "Oh, I wouldn't put ice in your Cab-er-nay...I just meant I'd put ice in mine, if I was to drink it."

VTM: "I hear they put ice in it in Para-gway" *(To self)* "Jesus, I'm getting screwed up...I'd better get out of here."

3rd BM: "Well, you guys would really like Ur-a-gway, if you were to go there." *—Many repetitions of this, plus a long discussion highlighting other South American attractions.*

VTM: *(Walking by businessmen on way out of bar)* "I've got to tell you guys—I've been to Ur-a-gway 12 times, and it sucks." *(Keeps walking)*

3rd BM: "Who the hell was that?"

2nd BM: "I never saw him before...some weirdo, I guess."

1st BM: "Only in America, right?"

- FADE -

A Feast of Reason

THE DEATH CERTIFICATE

SCENE

VTM in car headed for Santa Clara County (CA) Court House to obtain Certificate of Death of ex-wife, required by Lockheed Retirement Office in connection with payment of retirement benefits. He has procrastinated on this for over a week in order to psych himself up to come to grips with the County bureaucracy (with which he has had previous experience). Further, in the immemorial words of Steve Jerbic, he is "a little hung over, and easy to piss off."

CHARACTERS

- VTM
- Various County employees

VTM: *(To self)* "Jesus, this is going to be a pain in the ass. The whole County system is populated by people whose sole purpose in life is to stick their feet in the aisle when a guy wants to get something done—given that you can find one who speaks other than broken English in the first place."

Parks car four blocks away from Court House, hikes in and finds Records Department.

VTM: *(To clerk)* "How does a guy go about getting a Death Certificate?"

Clerk: *(In a tone that suggests that VTM is a simple shit)* "Oh, we don't keep Death Certificates *here*—for that, you'll have to go to the County Recorder's Office at First and Hedding."

VTM: *(To self, while leaving)* "I knew it...I frigging knew it was going to be a goddamned scavenger hunt. Why aren't Death

Certificates kept in the Records Department? It's a fucking record, isn't it? *All* records should be kept in the Records Department, or they should change the goddamned name of the place to '*Some* Records Department.'"

Continues to whip self into frenzy while hiking back to car. Drives to vicinity of First & Hedding; parks only three blocks from County Building; walks in, finds records place; and fills out "Blue Form"" in accordance with hand lettered sign taped to top of vacant counter.

After 5 minute wait, a female Hispanic clerk approaches counter—

VTM: *(To self)* "I fucking knew it—I knew that sooner or later I would draw one of these Taco Queens—though normally they are assigned only to answering questions over the telephone."

Through a combination of hand signs and pidgin English, VTM communicates to clerk his desire to obtain a Death Certificate.

Clerk: *(In flawless English)* "While we do issue Certificates of Death, we normally do not receive the certificates at this office until approximately 60 days after the death. Since this death occurred only about a month ago, we will not yet have the certificate. However, you can obtain a copy at the County Health Department, which is located adjacent to County Hospital on Bascom Avenue near Moorpark."

VTM: *(To self, while leaving)* "Health Department's ass...when do I get to talk to the frigging County Flood Control people? Dealing with these assholes is like dealing with Lockheed Central Procurement...they don't want to help you, they want to break your spirit, in the hope that you'll give up and go away, and they won't have to do any work." *(Again whips self into towering rage.)*

Drives to vicinity of County Hospital, walks requisite four blocks to Health Department parking lot entrance and is greeted by hand-lettered sign taped to locked door:

'PLEASE USE BASCOM AVE. ENTRANCE ON OPPOSITE SIDE OF BUILDING'

VTM: *(To self)* "I'm going to kill one of these Civil Service fuckheads before this is over."

Enters Bascom Avenue entrance into lobby completely devoid of personnel, signs, or instructions of any kind, but finally locates proper venue—

VTM: *(To clerk)* "I need a Death Certificate."

Clerk: "Do you have a Blue Form?"

VTM: "Yes, you're not even going to slow me down with that one."

Clerk: *(Takes and reads form, goes to filing cabinet three paces away, and instantly produces proper Death Certificate)* "This it?"

VTM: "Yes, but does your Supervisor know about this procedure?"

Clerk: "What procedure?"

VTM: "The issuance of a document with absolutely no delaying tactics, or even the slightest attempt at a rear-guard action. I would guess that your future with the County is shaky, at best."

OR, IS EVERYBODY NUTS BUT ME?

Clerk: "That will be $8.00, please."

Having pissed away the entire morning, VTM returns home, brings in mail, which includes a letter from the Lockheed Retirement Office stating the following:

"Dear Mr. Miller:

With reference to our letter of early February requesting a Death Certificate for your ex-wife, please be advised that we have obtained a certificate from another source; therefore, you are not required to furnish a Death Certificate..."

- FADE -

MAYBE IT'S ONLY AN EXPRESSION

SCENE

Bar at Tony Roma's, around 11:30 AM.

CHARACTERS

- Monica, lady bartender
- Jeff, a Tony Roma's regular
- Waitress (name unknown)
- VTM

Jeff: *(To waitress)* "Have you seen Mike and Sue lately? I haven't seen them around for a while."

W: "No, and to tell the truth, that's okay with me."

Monica: "Oh? Why is that?"

W: "Well, let's just say that the last time I saw Mike, he left a bad taste in my mouth."

- FADE -

OR, IS EVERYBODY NUTS BUT ME?

THE ALL-CONFERENCE GREETER

SCENE

Around 12:00 noon on a Friday, VTM receives a phone call at home from Emmett Taft.

CHARACTERS

- Emmett Taft
- VTM
- Loretta

ET: "Turn on Channel 11 at 5:00 this afternoon—I think I'm going to be on TV."

VTM: "Oh yeah? How is that?"

ET: "Well, as you probably know, the Smithsonian Institution Traveling Exhibition is opening in San Jose this weekend, and I've volunteered to be a greeter."

VTM: "A greeter? What the hell does a greeter do?"

ET: "He greets people at the door—tells them where the various exhibits are, answers questions, and so on."

VTM: "Jesus Christ, Taft, what the hell's the matter with you? The 'Grover Whelan♣' of Santa Clara, for Christ's sake…what causes you to do shit like this?"

♣ New York mayor Fiorello La Guardia's "Official Greeter" of visiting VIP's

A Feast of Reason

ET: "Well, I enjoy helping out on things when I can...anyway, Channel 11 News was in the exhibition hall this morning and videotaped a bunch of stuff, including an interview with me."

VTM: "Wonderful."

ET: "So be sure to turn on Channel 11 at 5:00 this afternoon."

—Around 4:00 PM, VTM reveals this conversation to Loretta; announces his intention to take a nap; and requests that she turn on the bedroom TV at 5:00 PM, and awaken him should Taft appear—

Loretta: *(At 5:01 PM)* "Wake up—the Channel 11 News is on, and they said in the lead-in that they're doing a feature on the Smithsonian Traveling Exhibition...so Emmy will probably be on."

—Following the initial commercial, the Channel 11 'newsperson' (surprisingly, not an Asian) announces that their first feature will be coverage of the Smithsonian Institution Traveling Exhibition. She goes on to note that this exhibition has been moving from city to city across the U.S., and further describes the diverse nature of the exhibits—specifically mentioning a 2 1/2 million year old moon rock, an early telegraph key, 'Kermit the Frog,' the Moon Rover vehicle, and the red shoes worn by Judy Garland in <u>The Wizard of Oz</u>. She also notes that many local people have volunteered to help with the exhibition—among whom is Mr. Emmett Taft of Santa Clara—Tape rolls:

ET: *(Peering owlishly into the camera)* "The Smithsonian Institution Traveling Exhibition is a wonderful thing, and everyone who can, should make it a point to visit the exhibition while it's in San Jose. The Smithsonian Institution belongs to all Americans, and this traveling exhibition provides a great opportunity for local people to view these amazing exhibits. It should be particularly rewarding to people who have never had a chance to visit the Smithsonian Institution in Washington, D.C."

VTM: "Jesus, is that it?"

L: Apparently so...you'd think that he would at least have tried to work in a plug for the Management Association."

VTM: "So I screw up my nap for a goddamn 10-second sound bite...'The Smithsonian Institution belongs to all Americans'– Jesus Christ, I'm going to frigging heave."

L: "At least he didn't use 'The Nation's Attic.'"

—VTM returns to nap, but cannot go back to sleep. After about 20 minutes, he gives up—still vaguely troubled by the Smithsonian news feature—

VTM: *(To Loretta)* "Who the fuck is 'Kermit the Frog?'"

- FADE -

A FOOL AND HIS MONEY

SCENE

Early December 1997, driving across Tulsa with Frank Westerman (an old Tulsa buddy) to attend a memorial service for a mutual old friend. VTM is modishly attired in a dark blue suit, Burberry raincoat, and navy blue rain hat.

CHARACTERS

- VTM
- Frank Westerman

FW: "So, where did you get the hat?"

VTM: "I got it in Wales...the last time Loretta and I went to Britain we drove up through Wales—which, incidentally, is about the prettiest countryside I've ever seen...especially the northern part of Wales. I thought Scotland was pretty—and it is—but north Wales is about the most beautiful thing you can imagine. Anyway, we stopped in this little village with an unpronounceable name, and I bought the hat in a small shop on the main street."

FW: "What did you pay for it?"

VTM: "I happen to remember the price...it cost exactly one pound."

FW: "They fucked you."

- FADE -

or, Is Everybody Nuts But Me?

RELATIVE TIME

SCENE

South Texas, where Frank Westerman has just returned from a short trip to Lubbock.

CHARACTERS

- Frank Westerman
- Friend

Friend: "I hear you just got back from the Panhandle...how long were you in Lubbock?"

FW: "I spent a month there one night."

-FADE-

THE CARE GIVERS

SCENE

Good Samaritan Hospital, San Jose, CA, where VTM has enrolled in Emergency Ward because of difficulty breathing. After a protracted examination involving many tests, doctors decide that VTM may have a mild case of pneumonia, or on the other hand (in the manner of MD's everywhere), he may not. In any case, it is decided that VTM should spend the night in the hospital on the old O_2 bottle. In keeping with this decision, he is transported by gurney (an indignity) to a double room on the third floor. The other occupant of the room is hidden by a curtain which separates the bed areas but, at the time of VTM's entry, he is engaged in a heated argument with a nurse over whether his blood pressure should be measured. VTM figures the guy is a weirdo, based upon his obvious inability to rationally support his argument. This view is later substantiated by the fact that the guy tends to make strange noises at random intervals. These noises (moans and shrieks) increase in frequency and intensity to the point that VTM can no longer tolerate the decibel level.

CHARACTERS

- VTM
- Others (many)

ACT I

VTM: *(to roommate)* "HEY FUCKHEAD, SHUT UP, FOR CHRIST'S SAKE.'

 —*Approximately 15 seconds of silence*—

Crazy
Guy: "Are you talking to me?"

or, Is Everybody Nuts But Me?

VTM: "You're goddamned right I'm talking to you."

CG: "Oh, Jesus, I'm sorry. I didn't mean to cause..." *(guy's voice trails off into muttering/mumbling)*

—Another 15 - 20 seconds of silence—

CG: *(in small voice, apparently to self)* "Anyway, I'm not a fuckhead."

—After about 15 minutes, the guy begins to moan and groan again, albeit in comparatively muted tones. Nevertheless, VTM has had a bellyful at this juncture, so gets out of bed and goes in search of Nurses' Station. Finds Nurses' Station, which encompasses six or seven female personnel who are armed with either keyboards, clipboards, or telephones—

VTM: *(using H-bomb voice)* "WHAT THE HELL IS THIS PLACE, THE GODDAMNED DE-TOX UNIT? THAT GUY YOU PUT ME IN WITH IS A FRIGGING NUT...WHO THE HELL CAN SLEEP IN THAT ZOO? EITHER GO SHOOT THE SONOFABITCH, OR GET ME ANOTHER ROOM!!!"

—Stunned silence—

VTM: *(to self)* "Apparently it's been some time since these broads have been exposed to the 'command voice.'"

Crew Chief Nurse: "What is your name, sir?"

VTM: "MILLER...TODD MILLER.'

CCN: "Yes, if you'll just go with Helen, Mr. Miller, she will get you situated in another room."

VTM: "I HAVE TO GO BACK AND GET MY GEAR."

CCN: "I'll help you with that, while Helen prepares the new room."

—At length, VTM is settled in another double room in which he is the sole occupant. His pleasure with the absolute quiet is somewhat tempered, however, by the fact that it is now 3:00 AM—

ACT II

—At 5:30 AM, VTM is awakened by blood pressure taker, reawakened 30 minutes later by blood extraction specialist, and in another 30 minutes by breakfast provider. At this point, VTM decides that sleep is out of the question, so lies stiffly on back, awaiting the next assault on his disposition; he does not have to wait long. Around 8:00 AM an older guy and his wife appear in the room with a nurse, who pulls the dividing curtain closed. VTM divines from the overheard conversation that the guy is in to get an irregular heartbeat straightened out—a procedure that, apparently, will take place in the room. The guy's main concern, however, is the fact that he stands to miss one or two days of bowling...much discussion ensues with his wife re: 'the league,' 'the guys at the lanes,' etc. VTM notes that God has singled him out once again.

VTM: *(to self)* "Bowling? Jesus Christ, first I get Crazy, now I get Square...I don't know which is worse."

or, Is Everybody Nuts But Me?

—Over the next hour, about 10 or 12 people appear in the guy's half of the room. From conversations heard over the curtain, VTM identifies voices as being the guy's daughter, one grandson, one granddaughter, two family friends, three bowling buddies, and several unknowns—

VTM: *(to self)* "Mother of God—the guy's made a fucking festival of the thing."

—Around noon, the guy's doctor appears to begin heart synchronization procedure. His first step is to run off the Mardi Gras Personnel—a definite plus. The procedure takes about an hour, after which:

Dr: "I'm finished now and your heartbeat is back to normal. Everything is fine...just take it easy and don't step in front of any trucks...Ha, ha."

Guy: "I'll sure try not to, Ha, ha."

VTM: "Jesus."

Nurse: "Well, everything is fine now...you're OK."

Guy: "Thank God."

Nurse: "Yes, God is on your side."

VTM: *(to self)* "I'm going to jump out of the fucking window."

Guy: "Yes, we all owe everything to 'The Man Upstairs.'"

VTM: *(to self)* "Mother of Christ...the guy's out of a WW II movie—it's a matter of time until he comes up with 'A Wing and a Prayer' or the thing about atheists in foxholes."

—Dr. and nurse leave, only to be replaced by bowling buddies bearing news from the lanes and, later, an Oriental orderly—

OO: *(To guy, after listening to conversation)* "You bowl? I also bowl. I bowl at Futurama Lanes one day a week. How often you bowl?"

Guy: "Only on days ending with a 'Y.'"

OO: "Days ending in 'Y'...why, that every day—Ho, ho, ho."

VTM: *(to self)* "By God, the slope is right on top if that one."

—Bowling conversation continues—now multicultural, owing to participation by OO—

VTM: *(to self)* "Jesus frigging Christ—I can't bear any more of this shit but, after all the hell I raised last night, I hate to ask them to put me back in with the crazy guy...Maybe I could just...."

- FADE -

OR, IS EVERYBODY NUTS BUT ME?

THE FEMININE MYSTIQUE

I summarize the contents of this section by quoting an unsung philosopher I once overheard in a saloon:

"No guy in America understands what goes on in a broad's head."

THE FEMININE MYSTIQUE

Honey Vanilla	153
Assertiveness Training 101	155
Hello Dolly	156
The Austin Connection	157
Trauma	158
The Ballad of Priscilla Cotter	162
The Marilyn Monroe Fan Club	165
Pick A Number	167

or, Is Everybody Nuts But Me?

HONEY VANILLA

SCENE

Express checkout line, Food Villa Market, Los Gatos, CA

CHARACTERS

- Young woman (YW) being checked out
- VTM - in line behind YW
- Checker - Also a female

YW: *(While writing check for three items)* "I notice that you never have any Haagen-Dazs plain vanilla ice cream in the freezer case back there."

Checker: "What?"

YW: "You never have any Haagen-Dazs plain vanilla...you always only have Haagen-Dazs Honey Vanilla."

C: "I didn't know that."

VTM: *(To self)* "Me neither."

YW: "Honey Vanilla is all right, but I like plain vanilla a lot better...do you suppose you can get some?"

C: "I'm sure we can...I'll talk to the Manager."

YW: "Honey Vanilla is okay, I just like plain vanilla better."

C: "I think the Ice Cream Man comes on Thursdays."

YW: "Honey Vanilla is just a different flavor—and I like plain vanilla better."

VTM: *(To self)* "I wonder why broads have to say the same thing 10 or 12 times?...maybe it's just part of their natural compulsion to talk."

C: "I'm sure the Ice Cream Man comes on Thursdays."

YW: "Well see if you can't get some plain vanilla...I like Honey Vanilla all right, but it's just not the same as plain vanilla."

Young woman picks up three purchases, checkbook, purse, and leaves.

VTM: *(To checker)* "How come all you have in the freezer case back there is Haagen-Dazs plain vanilla...I like Honey Vanilla, and you never have it."

C: "What?—I, um, thought that...."

VTM: "When does the Ice Cream Man come?"

C: "Oh! You heard me talking to that lady, didn't you? I know when someone's pulling my leg!"

-FADE-

or, Is Everybody Nuts But Me?

ASSERTIVENESS TRAINING 101

SCENE

Tao Tao bar, around 1:15 PM...lunch crowd is beginning to thin out.

CHARACTERS

- VTM
- Young woman and guy, about three stools away
- Bartender (Kingman)
- Others

VTM overhears following snatch (if I may be forgiven use of the term) of conversation:

Young
Woman: "Well, my boss has *really* intimidated me for a long time, but I've *finally* reached the point of self confidence and—um—assurance that I've learned to yell back at him...and that's what I really need to become a complete—um—*whole* person...."

VTM: *(To self)* "Jesus, you'd think that sitting in a saloon, a guy would be fairly safe from shit like this—but, hell no, those mothers are everywhere, anymore, etc., etc....*(to bartender)* Kingman, give me another bar napkin."

-FADE-

HELLO DOLLY

SCENE

VTM's house, around 6:00 PM on a workday evening, having a few shooters.

CHARACTERS

- VTM
- VTM's ex-wife (name forgotten)
- Jack Milton—An old Tulsa buddy from Douglas Aircraft days.
- Dolly—Jack's wife

Dolly: *(Suffering from a whiplash injury sustained in collision whilst backing up car on a major highway)* "Well, Jack, like I told the doctor today, it's not the double vision that bothers me so much as my inability to think straight."

Milton: *(Removing cigar from mouth)* "Jesus, Dolly, what the hell are you doing laying a problem like that on the doctor? The poor mother's only a neurosurgeon, he's not a fucking magician."

-FADE-

or, Is Everybody Nuts But Me?

THE AUSTIN CONNECTION

SCENE

Lockheed Austin Division, (just off of Ben White Blvd.), Austin, Texas.

CHARACTERS

- VTM
- Texas Secretary

VTM: *(To Dave Bently's secretary, seated immediately outside Bently's empty office)* "Do you know where Dave is?"

Tex Sec: "Dave Bently?"

- FADE -

TRAUMA

SCENE

In his first major mistake of the day, VTM decides to take a watch down to the jewelry store for repair. In doing this, he has overlooked the related salient facts that the jewelry store is in the middle of a huge shopping center, and it is also the middle of the Christmas shopping season. He becomes aware of this when he pulls into the shopping center parking lot and is instantly overwhelmed by festive lot decorations and an infinite number of women shoppers driving SUVs.

CHARACTERS

- VTM
- Women (many)

VTM: *(Upon pulling into shopping center parking lot)* "Aw, shit."

VTM (now committed) drops off watch at jewelry store and, on way back to car, notices a shop window display which contains an item that he figures might make a suitable present for Loretta. Upon closer inspection of the elaborate window display and the shop's name ("Briar Patch"), however, VTM ascertains that this place is, in fact, a boutique...the type of establishment to which he has never come closer than three first downs. VTM is of two minds with regard to entering such a place, his previous shopping experience having been limited largely to hardware stores, lumber yards, and used car lots. Also, there is the ever-present risk of being seen entering or leaving a place of this type. Nevertheless, in a burst of self-sacrifice, VTM decides to take the thing on, figuring he can run a quick opener and be in and out before significant damage is done to his emotional well-being; in this, he is mistaken.

or, Is Everybody Nuts But Me?

VTM: *(To self)* "'Briar Patch,' for Christ's sake."

Mentally associating himself with Alice and the rabbit hole, VTM enters the store and instantly finds himself in a female-contrived wonderland, i.e., he is knee deep in cute. There are baskets of all shapes, colors, and sizes; dolls, doll houses, covered bowls (some in the shape of chickens), cutting boards, wall and window hangings, a legion of stuffed animals (some clad in Santa Claus vestments), nine (by actual count) decorated full-size fake Christmas trees, serving dishes, cute trays, ceramic replica milk bottles emblazoned with flowers and humorous slogans (e.g., "Mad Money," "Our Nest Egg," "A Penny Saved is a Penny Earned"), cheese knives, jewel boxes, music boxes, and teapots (some covered by cloth garments, which VTM recalls having read somewhere are called "Cozy's"...he mentally excoriates himself for remembering this).

VTM: *(To self)* "Jesus Christ—Vagina City."

The store is, of course, populated solely by women—three sales people (persons?) who are identifiable by their Santa Claus hats, red vests, and reindeer earrings, and about seven professional shoppers. Owing to this, the air is filled with what VTM has come to think of as "Broadspeak." In this regard, he is almost instantly brought to his knees by two "simply darlings" and one "just the cutest thing ever."

Through this rain forest of conspicuous consumption (thank you, Thorstein Veblen) VTM spots his present, and moving deftly through a narrow opening between a Christmas tree and a large female shopper (who is apparently in a trance) grabs the item and summons one of Santa's Elves to effect the transaction.

SE: "My, that's certainly nice...is it a present?"

VTM: "Yes, it's for my wife."

SE: "I know she'll just fall in love with it."

VTM: *(To self)* "Why me, God?"

> *VTM completes transaction and exits boutique at a speed approaching that of light. Having been completely unnerved by this experience, he regains car and heads directly to Otto's Garden Room for a restorative adult beverage (or two). In his haste to gain the sanctuary of Otto's (and still visibly shaken) VTM unconsciously carries present into bar. He assumes seat on stool and immediately absorbs his next body blow of the day. Mike, the regular bartender, has been replaced by a young female bartender (YFB). In the celestial order of things, VTM regards female bartenders, along with female football sideline announcers, as being a plague visited upon an innocent populace.*

YFB: "What will you have?"

VTM: "Where the hell is Mike?"

YFB: "Oh, he's taking a few days off and I'm his temporary replacement."

VTM: "Wonderful."

YFB: "What can I bring you?"

VTM: "An Irish—up, no ice—Jamieson's if you have it, Bushmills if you don't."

YFB departs, returns with VTM's drink, and notices sack on bar.

YFB: *(Making conversation)* "What's in the sack?"

VTM: "It's a present for my wife."

YFB: "How cool...may I see it?"

VTM: "Sure..." *(removes present from sack).*

YFB: "Oh, wow! How totally adorable."

FADE

A Feast of Reason

THE BALLAD OF PRISCILLA COTTER

SCENE

On sidewalk outside Merrill, Lynch brokerage office, downtown Tulsa, circa 1949/50.

CHARACTERS

- VTM
- Ronnie Andrews
- Mary Cotter

RA: *(Looking into brokerage office through large front window)* "Jesus, look at that lovely thing sitting at the desk over on the left...she's the prettiest girl I've ever seen!"

VTM: (*(Looking through window)* "Yeah, that's Mary Cotter."

RA: "Goddamn! You mean that you actually know her?"

VTM: "Yeah, I've known Mary for years...she's Billy Cotter's sister. Billy and I went to Central High together."

RA: "Do you think you could line me up with her?"

VTM: "Yeah, probably—but I've got to tell you, Ronnie, that, intellectually speaking, Mary isn't your basic Chess Master."

RA: "I don't give a shit! Line me up, for Christ's sake...I'm in love!"

VTM: "Okay, but I don't want to listen to a whole lot of shit from you later on."

or, Is Everybody Nuts But Me?

RA: "Line me up! Line me up!

VTM enters brokerage office and approaches Mary's desk—

MC: *(At 90 dB, audio)* "TODD MILLER!! Where have you been all this time?"

VTM: *(To self)* "Jesus."

MC: "I haven't seen you in SIMPLY ages!!"

VTM: *(To self)* "Why do they always say 'simply'?" *(To Mary)* "Hi, Mary...I've been going to school down at Norman for the past few years, and I really don't get into town all that often anymore." *(Bullshit; he came to Tulsa every other weekend. ED.)*

MC: "Well, listen, let's get together. We could go out and..."

—Provides brief matrix of Tulsa night life Places to Go/Things to Do—

VTM: "Yeah, well, I'll give you a call the next time I'm in town, Mary, but right now, I'm on a somewhat different mission."

MC: "What do you mean?"

VTM: "Well, it's one of those 'I came to speak for Myles Standish' sort of things."

MC: *(Favoring VTM with Orphan Annie eyes look)* "Miles who?"

VTM: "Er, uh...Standish; Myles Standish...you know, John Alden, Priscilla, Myles Standish, and all that."

MC: "I don't know any John Alden, but—WAIT A MINUTE!!—is Miles Standish a Kappa Sigma?"

- FADE -

or, Is Everybody Nuts But Me?

THE MARILYN MONROE FAN CLUB

SCENE

Circa 1953–VTM and current girlfriend, Nancy Ogilvie, driving down 15th Street in Tulsa, on a Tuesday evening.

CHARACTERS

- Nancy O.
- VTM

VTM pulls up to stop sign and notes minor clatter in drive shaft.

VTM: *(Semi to self)* "Sounds like the U joints are worn...I'd better have that looked at."

Nancy O: "What are U joints?"

—In his first major mistake of the day, VTM attempts to explain the function of universal joints to a known girl.

VTM: "Well, did you ever see the underside of a car?"

NO: "Yes, I've seen my father's car up on a grease rack a couple of times."

VTM: "Well, you probably noticed a long tube running from the transmission to the rear axle. It's called a drive shaft, and it's purpose is to transmit power from the engine to the..."

NO: *(Interrupting)* "Look! They're having some kind of function over at the Methodist Church...I wonder what it is. Normally, weekly services are held only on Wednesday nights."

—VTM, being young and not yet fully aware of the genetic female microsecond attention span, doggedly presses on.

VTM: "...to transmit power from the engine to the rear wheels. The problem is that the connection cannot be rigid because..."

NO: *(Interrupting)* "Was that Patti Dunlap in that red convertible? It sure looked like her...I wonder who she's with?"

VTM: *(Becoming pissed at frivolous interruptions of weighty technical explanation, controls self and continues)* "...because when the car passes over an uneven surface the shaft must be able to flex. For this reason, U joints are placed at..."

NO: *(Interrupting)* "Look! Over at the Delman Theatre—Marilyn Monroe in 'Niagara.'"

VTM: *(Finally blowing top)* "Goddamit, Nancy, you're the dumbest frigging broad I've ever known."

NO: "Well what's the matter with you? *You're* the one who likes Marilyn Monroe."

- FADE -

or, Is Everybody Nuts But Me?

PICK A NUMBER

SCENE

VTM receives letter from American Express expressing concern that his newly issued Optima credit card has not been activated by telephone call. The letter also gives an 800 number to call in the event of any problem. VTM, who has never received the newly issued card, calls the 800 number to report this.

CHARACTERS

- VTM
- Next Available Customer Service Representative

> *The 800 number is answered by a computer, providing the usual menu of single digit-activated canned solutions. VTM punches the appropriate number and receives a recorded voice stating that all lines are busy, but to please stay on the line and his call will be answered by the "next available Customer Service Representative." This message is followed by a musical recording of several tunes, apparently randomly selected from an album of Lawrence Welk Favorites.*
>
> *At intervals, VTM is reassured that his call will be answered soon, but grows visably older while waiting for the next available Customer Service Representative (NACSC). At length, his call is answered—*

NACSC: "Good afternoon, my name is Cindi; how may I help you?"

VTM: "My name is Todd Miller. I received a letter from you people today expressing alarm over the fact that I have not called to activate my newly issued Optima credit card. The reason for this is that I never received the credit card."

NACSC: "I see. What is your credit card number?"

- FADE -

OR, IS EVERYBODY NUTS BUT ME?

A "P-DOCK" ANTHOLOGY

I have included this section as a sort of afterthought. It's about one of my great loves—boats*. I bought my first boat (a 16' outboard runabout) in 1967 and since then have progressed through several boats, until, in 1994, I achieved my ultimate dream—the acquisition of a 38' trawler yacht.

I berthed this boat ("Sashay") at the Pittsburg, CA, Marina in the San Joaquin River delta. This modern full service marina afforded all amenities needed/desired by boaters. Of greater interest, however, were the denizens of "P-Dock," where Sashay occupied berth P-10. Their presence gave rise to a number of conversations of cogency and depth, a few of which are presented here. This section, therefore, is dedicated to these intrepid mariners/accomplished raconteurs of "P-Dock," who established a new and lofty standard in the field of philosophical expression.

---

* This subject may not be of compelling interest to all readers but, screw it, it's my book and I get to write about boats if I want to.

A "P-DOCK" ANTHOLOGY

The Welcome Wagon	171
The Great Pie/Coffee/Carpet Caper	174
Aural Saturday	179
Rub-A-Dub-Dub	183
The Importance of Neutrality	188
Time, Temperature, Telephones, and Truck Lights	191

or, Is Everybody Nuts But Me?

THE WELCOME WAGON

SCENE

"P-Dock," Pittsburg Marina, Pittsburg, CA, on a Saturday morning in February. A guy named "Jimmy" (last name unknown) has recently moved his boat from old part of marina into slip adjacent to Emmett Taft's slip.

CHARACTERS

- Emmett Taft
- Jimmy
- VTM

ET: "I've got to go up to the boatyard and pay Frank for the work he did on my boat last week. Do you want to go with me?"

VTM: "Sure."

ET: "But first, I want to introduce myself to my new neighbor—I think his name's 'Jimmy.'"

VTM: "Bullshit, Taft, you can do your Dale Carnegie number later...let's go see Frank."

—*Taft and VTM start up dock to boat yard, but Taft sees man working on aft deck of boat next to his. Taft immediately stops and compulsively begins conversation—*

ET: "Hello there, my name's Emmett Taft, and I'm your neighbor in the next slip. I just wanted to stop by and introduce myself."

VTM: *(To self)* "Aw, for Christ's sake."

A Feast of Reason

New
Neighb'r: *(Semi-overwhelmed by this nuclear burst of good fellowship)* "U well...Hi...my name's 'Jimmy'...I just moved my boat in last week

ET: *(Continuing to project his George Babbitt/Rotary Club person* "Well, I heard you were coming, and I wanted to be among t first to welcome you aboard."

VTM: *(To self)* "Jesus Christ...the 'Grover Whelan' of 'P-Dock.'"

Jimmy: "Well, thanks, it's good to be over here in the 'high rent district Ha, ha."

ET: *(Wholly dedicated to the task of keeping the conversation goin* "I noticed that you backed your boat into the slip, Jimmy."

VTM: *(To self)* "Jesus...Ray Charles would have noticed that."

Jimmy: "Well, I guess I just forgot which end was supposed to go in firs Ha, ha."

ET: "Ha, ha, ha, ha...ha, ha."

VTM: *(To self)* "Mother of God."

ET: *(Giving no quarter)* "I see that you've stained your cock woodwork brown, and varnished it."

Jimmy: "Yes, and I'm getting ready to re-varnish it, but I can't do a more varnishing in this wet weather."

VTM: "I see that you've got it all sanded down already, though." *(. self)* "Goddamn, they've sucked me into this dumb conversation."

or, Is Everybody Nuts But Me?

Jimmy: "Yeah, I'm all ready to varnish, as soon as the weather turns nice."

ET: "Well, we've got to go up to the yard...I'll bring my wife by later and introduce her."

Jimmy: "That'll be nice...see you later."

—Taft and VTM move on up dock on way to boatyard—

VTM: "Taft, what the hell is the matter with you? Why are you always compelled to pull that Management Association shit? Jesus Christ, it's a goddamn addiction with you."

ET: "Well, it never hurts to be friendly and nice—and I, for one, believe that if more people took the time to be outgoing and courteous, the world would be a lot better place, and one in which we could all...."

- FADE -

A Feast of Reason

THE GREAT PIE/COFFEE/CARPET CAPER

SCENE

"P-Dock," Pittsburg, CA, Marina on a Saturday afternoon. VTM and Loretta have been invited aboard the CANADIAN SUNRISE, Frank and Maria Robinson's huge trawler, for homemade peach pie and coffee. In the spirit of inter-slip cooperation, Loretta has brought along a pot of coffee from the SASHAY. After the coffee pot is placed on the galley stove, the two couples assume seats in the salon for a pre-prandial discussion of the day's events.

CHARACTERS

- Frank Robinson
- Maria Robinson
- Loretta
- VTM

Maria: "I had originally intended to make a berry pie, but I came across this recipe for peach pie in an old cookbook I've had for years...It looked so good that I decided to make it instead of the berry pie."

Loretta: *(Observing the peach pie on the salon table)* "It sure looks like it's going to be good."

VTM: *(To self)* "Jesus."

—*At this juncture a tremendous crash occurs*—

Frank: "What the hell was that?"

VTM: "I don't know."

Maria: "My God the coffee pot exploded! Frank, I *told* you not to turn that burner any higher than low."

Loretta: *(Having viewed the calamity from her seat in the salon).* "No, it didn't explode, Maria...the stove top fell down on it."

Frank: *(Rapidly reassessing the guilt/blame factors)* "Didn't you secure the top with the rubber band?"

Maria: "I don't know, Frank, but...good Lord, look at that mess."

—All hands move to the galley where they observe a mixture of 12 cups of coffee and the remains of a shattered glass coffee pot on the galley deck. Fortunately, the galley carpet is completely covered by a rigid, transparent plastic sheet; nevertheless, coffee is beginning to seep into the carpet around the edges of the plastic. Panic begins to set in—

Maria: "Frank, get some towels or something so we can get the coffee up before it stains the carpet."

Frank: "Get off the plastic, Maria, and I'll pick it up and dump the whole thing over the stern."

Maria: "You can't do that, Frank."

Frank: "I can't do it with you standing on it."

—Frank is on knees, tugging at edge of plastic sheet; Maria holds position on top of sheet; coffee continues to seep into carpet; much shouting and gesticulating occurs—

VTM: *(To self)* "Jesus, where is Taft with the video camera when I need him?" *(to Frank)* "Frank, you'd better get the coffee up before you move the plastic sheet or you'll get coffee all over everything."

Frank: "OK, let's get the coffee up, then I'll dump the glass over the stern."

Maria: "You can't do that, Frank."

Frank: "Why not?"

Maria: "It just isn't right."

—Brief morality discussion ensues; coffee continues to seep; VTM has a bellyfull—

VTM: *(To Frank and Maria)* "If you'll both get out of the way, I'll clean up the mess. Maria, hand me that sink sponge."

Frank: "Don't use the sponge, use paper towels—you'll get glass in the sponge."

VTM: *(Assessing the value of the used sink sponge at around 25 cents, when new)* "Jesus, Frank, I'll buy you a new sponge...paper towels won't make a dent in this mess...but first I've got to get this glass up."

—Frank becomes sullen—

Frank: *(A doom-sayer of world-class ability)* "You'll cut yourself on the glass."

VTM: "I'm not going to cut myself, Frank."

—VTM does, in fact, nick little finger on first shard of glass, but is able to hide wound from Frank, and play through the pain.

or, Is Everybody Nuts But Me?

He cleans up remaining glass (Maria provides paper sack to ensure that glass does not go over the stern), and wipes up coffee with forbidden sponge—

Frank: "OK, let me get the plastic up, and I'll take it outside and clean it."

—Frank departs with plastic. With Frank gone, VTM grabs big (expensive) counter sponge and, with Maria's help, cleans coffee stains out of galley carpet. At length, Frank reappears, having left the plastic sheet on side deck to dry. All hands reassume seats in salon where a sense of calm begins to assert itself and, in time, the voice of the turtle is again heard in the land—

VTM: "Frank, I think I got all the coffee out of the carpet—so there should be no stains when it dries."

Frank: "Swell."

Maria: "Loretta, I'm so sorry about your coffee pot...I'll get you a new one."

Loretta: "No, Maria...forget about it...that was an old pot anyway."

Maria: "No, Loretta, I'll get you a new one."

Loretta: "No, Maria, we have at least four coffee makers at home, and I know that two of them are brand new—never been taken out of the box."

Maria: "I'd just feel better if you'd let me replace it."

Loretta: "No, Maria, that's an old coffee maker that I've been wanting to get rid of for years—but you know how Todd is—he uses things until they just fall apart."

VTM: *(To self)* "Jesus, how did I get to be the horse's ass...I thought I was the hero for cleaning up the mess."

—N additional iterations of the Maria/Loretta serve/volley coffee pot dialog occur—

VTM: *(To self)* "The way I understand the thing is that Maria wants to buy Loretta a new coffee pot, but Loretta doesn't want her to. On the other hand, maybe neither understands what the other is saying. Also, maybe I'm just getting irritable because I don't have a hand grenade to throw. Still, if I could just...."

- FADE -

or, Is Everybody Nuts But Me?

AURAL SATURDAY

– A TWO CHAPTER FARCE –

SCENE

A Saturday morning on VTM's boat at Pittsburg, CA, Marina. Owing to the fact that their wives have gone to a weekend dog show, VTM and Emmett Taft have temporarily thrown off the yoke of marital oppression, and are recovering from the gin/vodka debauchery of the night before.

CHARACTERS

- VTM (About 2/3 deaf)
- Emmett Taft (5/4 deaf)
- Sheila–VTM's ex-secretary, and close friend of both VTM and ET, dating from the time (some years before) when the three worked together—now retired to her original home in Manchester, MA.
- Nancy–VTM's girl cousin (known to VTM and ET as "Magnolia, The Flower of Southern Womanhood")–born and bred in the Commonwealth of Virginia but, with her husband Joe, a long-time resident of Ft. Worth, TX.

CHAPTER 1

THE DIRECTION FINDERS

VTM: "What is that buzzing noise?"

ET: "What buzzing noise?"

VTM: "For Christ's sake, can't you hear that?"

ET: "It's probably the refrigerator."

VTM: "Bullshit, Taft, it's not the refrigerator...I think it's coming from outside."

—VTM and ET step outside onto deck of boat—

ET: *(Points in a northwesterly direction)* "I think it's coming from over there."

VTM: "There's nothing over there but water. I think it's coming from that direction." *(Points due South.)*

ET: "No, it's more from over there." *(Points Southeast.)*

VTM: "Jesus, this is ridiculous—with the possible exception of Helen Keller, the two of us are probably the least qualified people on the face of the earth to make judgments on sounds of any type...and especially of their origin."

ET: "I still think it's somewhere over there...maybe a little more to the left, but maybe...."

- INITIAL FADE -

CHAPTER 2

THE VIRGINIA YANKEE

About an hour after the noise[*] episode, the boat phone rings— It is Sheila, responding to a message left on her answering machine by VTM the night before.

---

[*] The noise turned out to be a guy pressure washing his boat about six slips up the dock (due East).

VTM: *(Concluding a brief discussion of health and weather)* "Well, it's sure good talking to you, baby—I'm glad you got my message. Hold on a minute, though, Emmett wants to say hello."

ET: *(Launching immediately into an "out of nowhere" monologue)* "Barbara and I are going back to Oklahoma in November to see the OU–Colorado game. This will be our third trip back...normally, we fly into DFW, change planes, and fly to Oklahoma City. This year, though, we've decided to rent a car at DFW, and drive to Norman for the game."

VTM: *(To self)* "Why, in Christ's name, is he telling Sheila all this?"

ET: "On the way home, I thought maybe we would drop by and see you before we turn the car in at the airport."

VTM: *(To self)* "Jesus, I can't believe the mother's going to go from Norman, OK, to Ft. Worth, TX, by way of Manchester, MA...something's screwed up here." *(To ET)* "Who the hell do you think you're talking to?"

ET: "Magnolia."

VTM: "For Christ's sake, Taft, it's Sheila."

ET: "Sheila?"

VTM: "Sheila."

—*Another bizarre conversation ensues—this one even more surreal than its predecessor—during which each party attempts to explain what he/she thought during various phases of the earlier exchange.*

("Jesus, I'm sorry, Sheila, I thought that...; Well, I wondered why you....; I know it sounds funny, but you sounded like...; Well, I thought something was strange when you said....;" etc., etc., etc.)

VTM: *(To self)* "Mother of Christ...this is worse than finding noises."

—Mercifully, phone conversation finally ends—

ET: "God, I thought I was talking to Magnolia."

VTM: "Jesus, Taft, can't you tell the difference between Sheila's flat, grinding Boston accent, and Magnolia's Virginia ham-hock delivery?"

ET: "Well, they both speak softly and I thought that you told me it was Magnolia."

VTM: "Bullshit, I didn't tell you it was Magnolia...anyway, why would Magnolia be calling us on the boat? She doesn't know we're here, and would have no reason to call even if she did. Also, you will recall that we left a message for Sheila last night."

ET: "Oh yeah, I forgot about that...I sure thought I was talking to Magnolia, though."

VTM: "I'd like for you to go through the part again about swinging by Massachusetts in the rental car."

ET: "Fuck you."

- FINAL FADE -

or, Is Everybody Nuts But Me?

RUB-A-DUB-DUB

SCENE

A very cold, very foggy, and completely miserable January day in the Sacramento/San Joaquin river delta. Emmett Taft, VTM, and a yacht broker named Steve are moving a 32-foot twin diesel Bayliner power cruiser from the labyrinth of canals which comprise the community of Discovery Bay, CA, to the Pittsburg, CA, Marina—a circuitous water route of approximately 25 miles. The outside temperature is in the low 30's, and, owing to the tulle fog blanketing the entire delta area, visibility is in the order of 20 to 30 feet. The three mariners are aloft on the fly bridge where the forward portion of the enclosure has been removed in a vain attempt to increase visibility.

CHARACTERS

- Emmett Taft—partially deaf
- Steve—with rock crusher voice
- VTM—hungover and easy to piss off

Steve: *(Peering out over bow while manning the helm)* "Well, nothing ventured, nothing gained, I always say."

VTM: *(To self)* "Jesus."

ET: "What?"

Steve: *(Increasing volume of voice to threshold of pain)* "Nothing ventured, nothing gained!"

ET: "Oh."

VTM: *(To self)* "Christ—that mother's voice could etch glass at 50 yards."

Steve: "Well, maybe it'll clear off a little when the sun gets higher."

ET: "What?"

—Steve repeats at 120 db audio—

VTM: *(To self)* "This is going to be a lovely fucking day with old Leather Lungs bellowing every sentence at Taft two or three times."

The route taken from Discovery Bay follows Old River through Piper Slough, into False River, thence into the San Joaquin. As the route is progressed, visibility is reduced even more, and hypothermia begins to set in. About half way up False River, the port engine quits...much discussion ensues as to the cause of this misfortune—

Steve: *(After many attempts to restart port engine)* "I think the port engine is out of fuel."

VTM: "I don't know about that, but there's air in the fuel line and you can't restart without purging the line and priming the injectors."

ET: "What?"

VTM: "Nothing, fucking nothing."

—After about another ten minutes screwing around trying to start the port engine, it is decided to proceed using only the starboard engine. The problem here is that the fuel gage indicates that the starboard engine tank is also almost empty.

OR, IS EVERYBODY NUTS BUT ME?

After a brief fly bridge staff meeting (in which several opinions are aired) the decision is made to proceed slowly to the Antioch Marina (a distance of 8 to 10 miles) where diesel fuel can be had.

Steve: "I think we can make Antioch, but you never know."

VTM: *(To self)* "Jesus, Galen fucking Drake."

ET: "What?"

VTM: "He said you never know."

ET: "Who doesn't know?"

VTM: "I think they screwed you on the new digital hearing aid."

ET: "What?"

VTM: *(To self)* "At least, oncoming vessels won't have any trouble hearing our approach in the fog."

—The three mariners proceed slowly down the San Joaquin river on one engine. From time to time Taft assumes the role of fog lookout by placing his head squarely in front of Steve's line of sight from the helm. At length, he gives up and goes below—

Steve: *(About 10 minutes later)* "What happened to Emmett?"

VTM: "He went below."

Steve: "What for?"

VTM: "To measure the master berth mattress."

Steve: "Why, for Christ's sake?"

VTM: "The way I understand it, his wife gave him strict instructions to measure the master berth mattress...it has something to do with white sales, new sheets, or some frigging thing."

Steve: "New sheets? Jesus Christ, I just hope that we can make it to Antioch alive."

VTM: "Steve, that big cruiser that just went past is leaving a huge wake...you better turn into it."

Steve: "Right."

VTM: *(To self)* "I just hope that Taft won't be badly injured rattling around down below on the thick mattress in the padded master berth area...I've read that the combination of a rolling vessel and the knife-like exposed edge of a metal tape measure can be deadly."

—At length, the mariners make it into Antioch Marina where Steve does a masterful job of bringing the boat alongside the fuel dock on one engine. (At the same time, Taft's precision in measuring the mattress under adverse conditions cannot be overlooked.) After fueling up—and further fruitless attempts to start the port engine—the three seafarers proceed to the Pittsburg Marina (approximately 5 miles), where the boat is to be hauled in preparation for a marine survey—

Steve: *(After tying up at boatyard dock)* "Man, that was a hell of a trip...I sure wouldn't want to try that again...no way, Jose."

VTM: *(To self)* "Mother of Christ."

ET: "What did he say?"

VTM: *(Patience exhausted)* "He said that he's had a bellyfull of you and your shitty fucking hearing aid!"

ET: "Who has?"

- FADE -

A Feast of Reason

THE IMPORTANCE OF NEUTRALITY

SCENE

An April Saturday morning at Pittsburg, CA, Marina. Emmett Taft and other denizens of "P-Dock" are preparing to embark on the post-refurbishment maiden voyage of Taft's recently acquired 32-foot power boat (see <u>Rub-a-Dub-Dub</u>). All hands are preparing to cast off as the port engine starts; the starboard engine does not start.

CHARACTERS

- Emmett Taft
- Frank Robinson
- VTM & Loretta
- Frank Macaluso (owner of Vee Jay Marine Services—a boat yard adjacent to the marina)

ET: "I don't know what's wrong with the engine—it started right up this morning."

FR: "It sounds as though electrical power isn't getting through to the starter motor."

VTM: "Maybe the starter solenoid is stuck, or the main engine circuit breaker has popped."

Loretta: *(To self)* "Jesus."

FR: "It could be that the starter motor has jammed...let's see if we can turn the flywheel."

—*Frank Robinson disappears into the engine compartment below the aft deck and resets the circuit breaker, bangs on the side of the starter solenoid with a wrench, turns the flywheel by hand, and executes several other moves of quiet desperation...nothing works; the engine still wont turn over.*

A staff meeting is then held on the aft deck in which many postulations are advanced as to the probable cause of the malady, together with associated proposed solutions. Each individual's suggestion is listened to with respectful silence, accompanied by much wise nodding by the other members of the task force. The whole scene is a beautiful example of "guyness," i.e., a display of the things guys say and do when they don't have the vaguest clue as to the cause of a problem.

Meanwhile, Loretta has distanced herself from this pageant of masculinity by remaining in the main cabin, and, further, by adopting an obvious posture of increasing disbelief—

ET: "Well, I don't know what's the matter...the engine started OK this morning."

—More discussion—

ET: "I know, I'll call Frank (Macaluso) up at the yard—maybe he has some ideas."

—Taft enters main cabin, calls Frank on his cell phone, and describes problem—

FM: "Put the transmission in neutral." *—hangs up*

—Taft notices for first time that gear shift lever for the starboard engine is slightly off center. Returns lever to center position, turns key, and engine starts instantly. All hands join in a rousing cheer—

ET: "Goddamn, I feel like an idiot...I know an engine won't start unless it's in neutral...Jesus, what a stupid thing."

FR: *(A picture of compassionate camaraderie)* "Don't worry about it Emmett—it can happen to anyone."

ET: "Yeah, but it's so dumb."

VTM: "Don't sweat it Emmy...we all make mistakes like that from time to time—of course, a dialog will have to be written re the matter."

ET: "Aw, shit."

VTM: "No, really, Em, don't worry about it...it's not like you're going to remember this for the rest of your life—you will, however, remember it for the rest of *my* life."

ET: "I just can't figure out how I could have done such a dumb...."

– FADE –

or, Is Everybody Nuts But Me?

TIME, TEMPERATURE, TELEPHONES, AND TRUCK LIGHTS

-- A SOPHISTICATED DRAMA IN FOUR ACTS --

ACT I

SCENE

"P-Dock," Pittsburg, CA, Marina on a November Monday afternoon. After several hours of washing and cleaning up his boat (SASHAY), VTM boards Bob Long's boat (LA DOLCE VITA) in an adjacent slip for a restorative Bloody Mary and associated bullshit. After discussing–and solving–many of the nation's foreign and domestic policy problems, VTM and Bob Long turn their attention to local affairs.

CHARACTERS

- Bob Long –One of the great talkers of Pittsburg Marina who, in this regard, long ago attained the honor of "All-P-Dock." At the present time, if not "All-State," Bob is certainly "All-District."
- VTM

BL: "This morning, Frank Robinson took his boat (CANADIAN SUNRISE) up to Rio Vista to spend the night.

VTM: "That right?"

BL: "Yeah, but I noticed that Frank left his pickup lights on, up in the parking lot."

VTM: "I suppose the truck is locked."

BL: "Yeah, I tried the doors, but I think I'll give Frank a call on his cell phone."

VTM:	"What the hell can he do about it from Rio Vista?"
BL:	"Well, he at least ought to know about it—anyway I'm one of the few people who have Frank's cell phone number, but it's at home so I'll have to wait until I get home to give him a call."
VTM:	"I didn't know that Frank's cell phone number was classified."
BL:	"Well, he called me one time on his cell phone, and I just happened to write the number down…but it's at home."
VTM:	*(To self)* "The way I see it, Bob will call Frank from home, so that Frank can't do anything about his truck lights…on the other hand…."

- FADE -

ACT 2

SCENE

"P-Dock," Tuesday afternoon. Frank and Maria Robinson, having returned from Rio Vista, secure the CANADIAN SUNRISE in her slip and come aboard SASHAY for a debriefing/activity report.

CHARACTERS

- VTM
- Frank Robinson—Probably the premier conversationalist in the Pittsburg Marina—certainly "All-State" and, maybe, "All-West Coast." Frank is noted for his attention to detail which, while admirable for its precision, often leads to long convoluted digressions.
- Maria Robinson—Frank's deified wife

or, Is Everybody Nuts But Me?

- Loretta—VTM's sainted wife
- Cooper—Loretta's Golden Retriever

VTM: "So how was the trip?"

FR: "Absolutely perfect. The Sacramento River was like a mill pond both ways, there was no wind, and the weather was just gorgeous."

VTM: "That's great, Frank. Somehow, that never happens to me when I go out."

FR: "The only problem was last night...It was colder[*] than hell. We went into town for about an hour, and..."

—At this point, Frank pauses, looks silently upward into the middle distance, and mentally weighs the accuracy of his introductory clause. This characteristic is well known to all who know Frank—

"...no, it was more like an hour and ten minutes."

VTM: *(To self)* "We need an atomic clock here."

FR: "Anyway, when we got back to the boat, the temperature had dropped to around 55 degrees *(Again, the pause/moment of reflection)*, no it was more like 57 degrees. Well, to make a long story short[*], I turned on one of the boat heaters and we went to bed."

---

[*] Together, Frank and Maria Robinson weigh around 180 pounds; thus any temperature below 80° F is regarded by them as being "cold."

[*] Never in the annals of recorded history has Frank Robinson ever "made a long story short." On the other hand, going in the other direction, he can take a short story and...etc.

VTM: "So, how did you make out?"

FR: "Well, it was OK. I got up around three o'clock in the morning and the inside temperature had risen around 5 degrees—no, maybe 6 degrees—no probably more like 5 degrees."

VTM: *(To self)* ""Frank seems to be unsure here...I have to wonder what level of confidence one can reasonably associate with either figure."

Maria: *(Mercifully)* "Loretta, why do you have that ice chest on top of the dock steps?"

Loretta: "That's to keep Cooper from getting off the boat. He's learned how to get off the boat by himself...he got off the boat at the dock party last summer, and yesterday he did it again—so I put the cooler on the top step as a barricade."

M: "I had the same problem with Charlie[♦]. When he was a puppy, we lived in this two-story condominium in San Jose. We didn't want Charlie coming upstairs at night, so I put this big cardboard box on the second or third stair step to block him."

L: "Yes, that's how I use that cooler."

M: "Well, anytime we wanted to keep Charlie out of anywhere, I used that box and it always worked."

L: "Yes, they're very smart...it doesn't take them long to learn."

[♦] Maria's Golden Retriever, now deceased.

or, Is Everybody Nuts But Me?

VTM: *(To self)* "I'm going to frigging jump overboard...I believe I can clear that cooler on the top dock step by at least a foot."

FR: "Did I tell you about leaving my truck lights on?"

VTM: "No, but Bob Long told me yesterday."

FR: *(Undeterred)* Well, we were up in Rio Vista on the boat when the cell phone rang. Very few people have my cell phone number, and I almost never leave the phone on."

VTM: *(To self)* "Here's the thing about the cell phone number again."

FR: "I Just happened to have the phone on because Maria was expecting a call and about five minutes after I had turned it on *(pause, reflection)* no, probably more like 10 minutes later, lo and behold, the phone rang!"

VTM: *(To self)* "I'm on the edge of my seat."

FR: "It wasn't Maria's call, but Bob Long calling from home to tell me that I'd left my truck lights on."

VTM: "So, what did you do?"

FR: "Well, first I called Sam and Lorey, and they weren't home, then I tried Mac and Nancy and they weren't home either. Finally, I got ahold of Aeino and Marian, and asked Aeino if he would stand by the Marina gate to let a Triple A truck in. He agreed, so then I called the Triple A♣."

VTM: "And?"

♣ The couples mentioned are people who live aboard their boats at the marina.

FR: "Well, Aeino said that the Triple A truck got there in about 15 minutes *(pause),* yeah, that's about right, and that the Triple A guy got into the truck and turned off the lights in five minutes flat!"

VTM: "*(To self)* "A guy's got to admire Aeino's unalloyed, unconditional declarative statement of *'five minutes flat'.*"

(To Frank) "Did the truck start OK?"

FR: "I don't know—I haven't tried it yet."

- FADE -

ACT 3

SCENE

"P-Dock," Wednesday morning. As a result of his slavish adherence to Miller's First Law *('If one of anything is good, then five or six will be sensational.')*, VTM has OD'd on laxative pills the night before, thus is moving smartly up the dock toward the marina head in the parking lot. His next-to-worst fear is realized when he meets Bob Long halfway up the dock. Bob is accompanied by a tall man of middle years who assists Bob in blocking VTM's path to the head.

CHARACTERS

- VTM
- Bob Long
- Dick Baldwin

BL: "Hey, Todd, how's it going?"

OR, IS EVERYBODY NUTS BUT ME?

VTM: "Going well Bob—how you doing?"

BL: "Doing good...Todd, this is Dick Baldwin. Dick bought Harry's boat (PRIMA DONNA) and is new to "P-Dock."

DB: *(Draws a deep breath and, without ever breathing again, reveals the following):* "While new to 'P-Dock,' he is an old marina hand; was the first tenant in the new basin (where 'P-Dock' is situated), having moved his boat in before the basin was legally open, because fire hoses had not yet been installed; and they didn't even charge him any berth rent the first month."

VTM: *(To self)* "Jesus, this guy sounds like a legitimate contender for the 'P-Dock' Conversational Crown...although, several months must elapse before meaningful stats can be compiled."

BL: "Did I tell you about Frank Robinson leaving his truck lights on?"

VTM: "Yes, that subject has been touched upon."

BL: "Well, Frank was on his boat up in Rio Vista when I noticed that he'd left his truck lights on, and...."

—By this time, VTM is standing first on one foot and then the other, seriously alarmed by rapidly increasing internal pressure—

BL: "Now, I'm one of the few people who happen to have Frank's cell phone number, so...."

—VTM, in a final desperate move, puts a head fake on Bob Long, cuts back through the crease thus opened between Bob

A Feast of Reason

and Dick Baldwin, and breaks into the open field leading to the marina head. By tensing both buttock muscles, VTM is able to stiff-leg it across the parking lot to the head, a journey in which a gastro-intestinal accident of cataclysmic proportions is narrowly averted—

-- FADE -

ACT 4

SCENE

"P-Dock," Wednesday afternoon. VTM has just completed a day of sanding and varnishing the external teak on the SASHAY. He has boarded LA DOLCE VITA for the daily ration of Bloody Marys and bullshit.

CHARACTERS

- VTM
- Bob Long

VTM: "Jesus Christ, I've had a bellyful of that goddamned sanding and varnishing."

BL: "Yeah, keeping up a boat is a pain in the ass."

VTM: "I think I've got it down to about six or eight more days though, and then I'll be finished."

BL: "I bet you'll be glad of that...Say, did you hear about Frank Robinson leaving his truck lights on? Well I just happen to have his cell phone number at home, so I...."

- FINAL FADE -

AFTERWORD

Once again—"Is everybody nuts but me?"

OTHER BOOKS AVAILABLE FROM SHANNON ROAD PRESS
www.shannonroadpress.com

MAN UNDER, Brian Shaughnessy
> A gritty and gripping police procedural detailing the serial murders of homeless victims on the NYC Subway System.

CYPHER, Loretta Scott Miller
> A three-generation detective agency, operating out of an old church in Santa Cruz, CA, juggles motor yachts, stolen computer encryption, and drugs all in one case. Second in the ANADARKO GRACE series.

OUT FROM UNDER, Brian Shaughnessy
> Now in the Major Case Squad, the detectives from Brian Shaughnessy's first book, MAN UNDER, are faced with the unlikely prospect of having the ghost of an NYFD hero of 9/11 for a murder suspect.

LITTLE SISTERS, VOLUME I, collected by Loretta Scott Miller
> An anthology of mystery short stories showcasing the talents of nine new mystery authors.

BLIND PUPPY FIVE DOLLARS, A Joyous Memoir of a Rescued Golden Retriever, Loretta Scott Miller
> While no smarter or more beautiful than the majority of golden retrievers, Cooper was weird, odd, crazy and extraordinarily goofy. He knew how to have a good time and made me laugh every day.

www.ingramcontent.com/pod-product-compliance
Lightning Source LLC
Chambersburg PA
CBHW031245290426
44109CB00012B/437